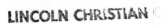 

THE LEADERSHIP LIBRARY
VOLUME 1 4
SECRETS OF STAYING POWER

Other books in THE LEADERSHIP LIBRARY

Well-Intentioned Dragons by Marshall Shelley

Liberating the Leader's Prayer Life by Terry Muck

Clergy Couples in Crisis by Dean Merrill

When It's Time to Move by Paul D. Robbins, ed.

Learning to Lead by Fred Smith

What Every Pastor Needs to Know about Music, Youth, and Education
   by Garth Bolinder, Tom McKee, and John Cionca

Helping Those Who Don't Want Help by Marshall Shelley

Preaching to Convince by James D. Berkley, ed.

When to Take a Risk by Terry Muck

Weddings, Funerals, and Special Events
   by Eugene Peterson, Calvin Miller, and others

Making the Most of Mistakes by James D. Berkley

Leaders by Harold Myra, ed.

Being Holy, Being Human by Jay Kesler

THE LEADERSHIP LIBRARY

Volume

Secrets of Staying Power

*Overcoming the
Discouragements of Ministry*

Kevin A. Miller

Carol Stream, Illinois

WORD BOOKS
PUBLISHER
WACO, TEXAS

WORD, CANADA
RICHMOND, B.C.

SECRETS OF STAYING POWER

©1988 Christianity Today, Inc.

A Leadership/Word Book. Copublished by Christianity Today, Inc. and Word, Inc. Distributed by Word Books.

Cover art by Paul Turnbaugh.

Library of Congress Cataloging-in-Publication Data

Miller, Kevin A., 1960–
    Secrets of staying power.

    (The Leadership library ; v. 14)
    1. Clergy — Office.   2. Clergy — Psychology.
I. Title.   II. Series.
BV660.2.M49   1988   253'.2   88-2854
ISBN 0-917463-19-6 :

Printed in the United States of America

To Karen,
who helped give me
the staying power
to write this

CONTENTS

INTRODUCTION

One of the first pastors I interviewed after coming to LEADERSHIP Journal told me of hiring a staff member who, unknown to him, was a pathological liar. The resulting uproar in the church — and accusations aimed at the pastor—caused him to go through the most painful, discouraging moments in his life. His case was unusual, so I assumed the accompanying discouragement was as well.

Then I talked with a pastor whose church had gone through a painful split due to a few difficult members. Another who felt he had met every challenge in his church and yet saw no exciting opportunities elsewhere. A third who had worked hard in his church for over a decade but had seen little growth.

Discouragement, rather than being a rarity, was, as John Stott has said, an "occupational hazard of the Christian ministry." Luther knew it; so did Spurgeon; so do most pastors today.

Thus, *Secrets of Staying Power*. This book is for those pastors who know the great joys and victories of the ministry but also candidly admit to times of discouragement. It's for pastors who want to overcome those periods and build an enduring ministry.

In keeping with the mandate of THE LEADERSHIP LIBRARY, the book asks not ethereal, philosophical questions but down-to-earth, practical ones: What aspects of ministry are most likely to cause pastors to feel discouraged, to want to give up? What can be done about them?

Also in keeping with previous volumes in THE LEADERSHIP LIBRARY, the book relies on the hard-won wisdom of working pastors. Virginia Vagt and Hope Grant of the research division of Christianity Today, Inc., developed and distributed a survey to 500 pastors randomly selected from the LEADERSHIP subscriber list. They then computer-tabulated responses and analyzed trends among the 170 surveys returned; the resulting information shaped in great measure the pages that follow.

I'm also indebted to the several dozen pastors who agreed to be interviewed in depth. In some of their stories, names and identifying details have been changed to preserve the privacy of people involved, but all are real. They show the wisdom, grace, and fortitude necessary to persevere in pastoral ministry. Each of these ministers has demonstrated a firm knowledge of the secrets of staying power.

O N E

THE UNBOUNDED AFFLICTION

The company of the discouraged is not an exclusive club, but it is a costly fellowship.

BRUCE W. THIELEMANN

Discouragement in ministry knows no bounds. It spreads across denominations, regions, and ages. It strikes seminarians and seasoned pastors alike.

And it can devastate pastors and their ministries. "Regardless of what we believe about the strength of God or perseverance of the saints," admits a Presbyterian pastor who's struggling with discouraging times himself, "discouragement breaks some people. They leave the ministry. And it's not sufficient to say they were never called. They were simply too discouraged to keep going."

That applies, sadly, to even the most experienced, hardworking, and energetic pastors, as Roger Landis, a pastor in the Midwest, discovered. Though names and identifying details have been changed to protect the people involved, the following account is based on true events.

Roger Landis had been a pastor for a long time — thirty-five years, in fact — but in all those years he'd never seen a search committee interview go more smoothly. It seemed that everything this Indiana church was looking for, he fit.

"We want more Bible teaching and less evangelism," Buck,

the head of the search committee, said. "Pastor Fraley was a wonderful man, gifted in evangelism. Never a service went by without an invitation. But now, with all the new Christians we've got in the church, we need somebody who's strong in teaching and preaching, who can guide them in Christian living."

"Well," Roger began slowly, considering his words carefully, "Bible teaching would have to be my forte, I'd say. I have led people to the Lord, but evangelism is not my primary gift. I love nothing better than to study and preach God's Word."

Roger looked around the table, and heads were nodding. Buck smiled at him. "We could tell that from listening to some of your sermons on tape," he said, and then, looking at the others, "Really enjoyed those, didn't we?" Heads nodded again.

This feels more like a family reunion than an interview, Roger thought to himself. He knew before the meeting was over that if the call came, he'd jump at it.

Sure enough, two weeks later he got a call from Buck. "The vote was unanimous, Roger. One hundred percent. The congregation can't wait for you to come."

"That makes two of us," Roger said. "I'm ready to go to work."

And go to work he did. Roger would go in to the office early — before seven, usually — and not get home till nine or ten at night. He'd never worked harder, but he had never had more energy, either. The congregation invigorated him in every way. Visitation, counseling, preaching — he was enjoying it all. "It's unreal," he told his wife, Jeanne. "I'm having so much fun here, when I go to sleep at night, I can hardly wait for morning to come."

Kaneville Community Church now had 160 members, but attendance was running a solid 235. The thing that excited Roger, though, was the potential for growth. The church had good attendance at midweek and on Sunday night, a strong Sunday school, an active youth group, boys' and girls' clubs

— it was waiting to explode. *If there's any church that will make it past the 200 barrier, it's this one,* he thought to himself.

Roger and Jeanne got close to the people quickly. They didn't realize how much the Kaneville people had become their family until March. That was when they had to face the deepest tragedy of their lives. Early one morning they were awakened by a phone call from Sgt. John Kraybill of the Pennsylvania State Police. Their son, he said, had been driving on Highway 196 when his car slid off the road and struck an embankment. "I'm sorry to report this, Reverend Landis, but he was killed immediately."

He was going to be twenty-two in a couple of weeks! Roger thought, but he was too stunned to cry. He just said "Thank you" quietly and hung up the phone.

Roger and Jeanne sat on the sofa and held each other until 6 A.M., when they decided it was late enough to call Harold, the church chairman.

"Oh, Roger, I'm sorry. I don't know what to say," he said. But in the next half hour two people came by with checks to help them with expenses for the trip. "Anything you need, we'll take care of," they said. The prayer chain went into action, and several ladies came to help Jeanne make last-minute arrangements for the trip east. So many people called or stopped by to express their sympathies that finally they had to ask them to stop so they could get some rest.

Roger was proud of his people. They knew how to put Christian love into action. As they drove along the Indiana Turnpike, a trip they'd hoped to make in May for Tim's Penn State graduation, Roger talked to Jeanne about it. "I wish they could come with us, Jeanne. I need those people. They're our family now."

Jeanne agreed. "We've been here only eleven months, but it feels like a lot longer than that. They've rallied around us."

Roger was glad to get back home after the funeral. He wanted to be back with the church people, and he wanted to get back to work to take his mind off Tim's death. The extra energy he expended began to pay off. Roger didn't give an invitation every Sunday, because he knew his congregation well enough to know when that was appropriate, but the times he did, people responded. It was exciting to lead some people to the Lord. Several new families joined the church in just a couple of months. By May, they were pushing 300 on Sunday morning.

"Maybe it's time to start thinking about a building program," Buck said at the May deacons' meeting. The board decided to bring in a denominational consultant to help them decide how to respond to the rapid growth. After two days of meetings and study, the consultant strongly recommended the church move to two services as soon as possible. "Your sanctuary's already well over 80 percent full," he said, "and at that point people stop coming because they don't like to be crowded. Without two services, you'll risk losing your momentum." The board agreed.

The consultant and Roger met together in Roger's office after the meeting. "I'll tell you one thing," the consultant said. "You are really making things move here, Roger."

"I don't think I'm being naive when I say this," Roger responded, "but I'm beginning to think this is the perfect church. In thirty-five years of ministry in all kinds of situations, I've never felt happier."

In August they made the switch to two services, and shortly after that Roger began hearing things, little things. Ellie, an older parishioner, said to him at the door one Sunday, "It just isn't the same coming at 8:30, Pastor. I miss seeing all my friends." Later, during the coffee hour, he overheard two ladies saying something like, "I never get to see you any more. I feel like we're losing our closeness as a church," and the other woman whispered, "When Pastor Fraley was here, it was like one big happy family."

Roger couldn't quite understand the comments. He'd led churches to almost double their size and never heard any complaints. And the church had said they were open to growth and wanted that. *They could always switch services once in a while if they want to see their friends,* he thought. *But maybe this is that psychological barrier above 200 they talk about.* Roger pushed the thought aside because at this point it didn't matter. If they went back to one service now, they'd be stacked on top of each other's shoulders.

By November Roger was starting to feel the need for some help. With his seventy-five-hour weeks, he'd been able to keep up with the growth, but now it was pushing beyond even that. He didn't need someone full-time, he thought, just someone who could give him twenty or thirty hours and take over the visitation and evangelism. That would keep the growth moving and free him up to concentrate on preaching. When Roger suggested hiring someone to the board, they approved it unanimously, and they found someone before three months had gone by.

Two weeks after the new associate started, Buck's wife invited Jeanne out for lunch, which Roger felt good about. Buck was influential in the church, so it was healthy to keep that relationship strong. But at two o'clock Jeanne called him at the office, not her usual practice.

"What's up, Honey?" Roger asked.

"Rita told me at lunch that there are a bunch of people from the church who are really disgruntled, about seventeen families, she thinks. They planned a secret meeting for next Tuesday. Rita found out about it because they invited her and Buck. But when she found out you and I weren't going to be there, she said she couldn't make it. She said she's really worried about it. Well, I am, too, Roger. I didn't know what to say to her."

"Not much you can say," Roger said tensely. "I'm just glad Buck and Rita told us about it ahead of time. I'll try to find out what's going on."

Roger hung up and then punched in the number for Warren Fraley, his predecessor. Warren had moved to a denominational post, and Roger had built a good working relationship with him. Right now Roger needed to talk to someone who understood the situation but wasn't directly involved.

"I was afraid something like this might happen," Warren said quietly after Roger had described the situation.

"What do you mean?" Roger demanded.

"Well, about a year before I left there, I started sensing something wasn't quite right. But I could never put my finger on it. There wasn't any blatant sin, just some friction that kept recurring."

"Friction?"

"I don't know if that's the right word, but something was going on between Buck, Dominic, and Bert Kelsey."

Oh, great, Roger thought. *Two deacons and a trustee — nobody major, just half the leadership in the church.* "What was going on between them?"

"Pushing and pulling, wanting to be in charge. I guess you could call it a power struggle. I kept thinking it would blow over. After all, it was only natural for three people who wanted to be pastors to try to assert themselves."

"They all wanted to be pastors?"

"Yes. Buck was a Roman Catholic brother, then left the order, married a nun, and eventually they both left the Catholic church to join Kaneville. But he's always had a yearning for church leadership."

"I never knew that," Roger said.

"And Dom and Bert attended either Bible college or seminary with dreams of becoming pastors. But in both cases, they had to give it up because of family pressures."

"So Dom and Bert are behind the meeting, and Buck felt ousted, so he blew the whistle?" Roger tried to piece it all together.

"Could be, but with Buck you're never too sure. He's a sweet guy, but sometimes what he says doesn't match what he does."

Roger was floored. *I guess I was naive,* he thought as he hung up. He was astonished that he hadn't heard anything earlier.

He spent the next three days on the phone, trying to find out whatever he could. It was the most awkward thing calling people without knowing what they knew, and them not knowing what he knew. He felt like a spy playing diplomatic cat-and-mouse. But gradually, after talking with Bert, Dominic, Buck, and others, he began to see that Warren had been right on target. The three were at the heart of the controversy.

Through the phone calls Roger found out what was driving the discontent. "There's not enough evangelism in the pulpit — that's what people are saying to me," Buck told him. "When Warren was preaching we used to see souls saved every Sunday. They felt good about that."

"But I thought people wanted less evangelism and more teaching now," Roger said.

"Well, the Lord calls us to go into all the world, Roger. That's not something we can put on the shelf."

Roger couldn't believe this was the same Buck who had told him they wanted a teacher and not an evangelist. But he decided not to get into a battle on the phone. "So evangelism is what people are upset about?"

"Yes, that and people say they're not being fed on Sundays. They need the meat of the Word."

"We're not being fed." What do you say about that? Ironically, this past Sunday one lady had told Roger, "We get so much from your sermons."

Through Roger's calls, word got out that the pastor knew about the meeting, and the plans for it fell through. Roger couldn't feel relieved. He didn't know how or when the discontent would surface again. For the first time, Roger began to feel tired at the end of a day.

Things stayed quiet for a month or so, and Roger tried to push ahead. The church hired a youth director, a young, energetic guy fresh from seminary. Roger felt good about having more support, and he knew a good youth ministry would help solidify the church's base of middle-aged parents.

Two weeks later Marie, an outspoken woman in the congregation pulled Jeanne aside. "Jeanne, that new youth director has got to go."

"Didn't you vote for Todd?" Jeanne asked.

"Yeah, I did. But I don't think he's the man."

"What's the problem?" Jeanne asked.

"He's just got to go," Marie said, her hands on her hips. "We've got to get rid of him. The kids don't relate to him."

"That's a valid concern," Jeanne said, "but don't you think it's a little early to tell? He's been here only two weeks."

Marie could see she wasn't getting anywhere, so she turned around and left.

When Jeanne told Roger about it that night, Roger couldn't help but get angry. "The poor kid hasn't even gotten his shoes off yet. I wish they'd just give people a chance."

The next few weeks felt lighter. Roger really enjoyed working as a team with Todd and his other associate. He got several compliments on his preaching, and he felt things in the church were back on track.

But then twice, just a couple of days apart, he overheard people talking in the hall about "the situation in the church." They'd stop talking and smile at him as he went by, but Roger caught enough to know the problems were starting again. He wanted to take action, but he didn't know what or where to attack first.

The building tension kept Roger awake some nights. It was all just beneath the surface, like a giant Loch Ness monster. He'd see the water foaming and bubbling, or get a glimpse of some bumps coming up, but the slimy thing would never surface so he could see what he was dealing with. He decided he needed a fresh perspective, so he set up a lunch with Dick Berger, his district superintendent.

"Boy, that upsets me to hear all that," Dick said, motioning to the waitress to bring more coffee.

"Am I doing something wrong?" Roger asked him. "I mean, how are you supposed to deal with this stuff?"

"You can't — at least, not right now. That church has always had an overgrown grapevine, but that's not exactly something you can call 'sin' and bring discipline for. The biggest problem, as I see it, is you've got a lot of immature leadership. They haven't learned about Christian submission yet."

"But why is the leadership so immature? Warren had a good ministry there." Roger looked Dick in the eye.

"Yes, but a year or two before you came, when they started the daughter church up north, they commissioned forty people to go up there and get it going. And just by chance, mostly, that group included some of the strongest leaders in the church. It left Kaneville with something of a lay leadership vacuum."

So that's why the power struggle began then, Roger realized. He came away from the lunch understanding things better, but feeling worse than before.

At the church, Roger was spending a lot of hours in counseling, which normally he enjoyed, but lately he'd had a string of highly emotional and probably neurotic individuals. It was beginning to wear him down. He didn't have a formal degree in counseling, but he'd taken a number of workshops and seminars over the years and had developed an effective approach. But this latest batch of people didn't seem to improve no matter what he said or did.

The worst one was a woman named Marybeth. Her problems were numerous and recurring. One week it was her insensitive husband, the next week it was her relationship with her aging dad, the next it was her feeling that nobody respected her opinion. The concerns all seemed valid at first, but they were like spiders' webs — they looked big, but they were flimsy and strangely sticky. After a couple of months with not the slightest trace of improvement in Marybeth, as far as either one could see, Roger tried to be as direct as he could. "Marybeth," he said, "I care about you very much, and because of that I want you to get the best help you can. Since I've been seeing you for some time and you haven't noticed any improvement, I'd like to refer you to a professional counselor for whom I have high regard."

"Oh, no, Pastor, I'm getting so much from you," Marybeth said. She was adamant about not switching. Roger thought,

Well, if she really wants to work at it, I hate to turn her away, and he set up another appointment.

But after two more sessions, they were back to square one. Roger was getting discouraged. He tried to be as frank as he could. "Marybeth," he said, "I've given you everything I know, and I think that for your benefit a professional counselor is the next step. Your problems seem to be beyond my expertise."

"No, Pastor," she said, "I want to stay. I feel like you've helped me get close to a breakthrough."

Roger felt stuck. He really did not want to see her anymore; he obviously wasn't helping. But if he refused to see her until she went to a professional, he'd create large political waves through the congregation. Marybeth was the kind who could blow something out of proportion; that was one of her problems. If there was anything Roger didn't need, it was more turmoil. So he agreed to see her one more time.

Roger was always careful to take Mondays off, and he began to really look forward to them. Often he and Jeanne would get away from the house and take a hike in the woods. They'd talk things out as they went along, and usually by lunch Roger's spirits would start to lift again.

"I don't know, Jeanne," he said as they sat down on a large fallen tree and zipped open their daypacks. "Lately I've been going to bed tired, but I'm not sleeping well, and then I get up tired. I have to push myself to get through almost every day."

"I've noticed that, Honey, and it worries me."

"But I can't figure out why. I love being a pastor, and I know I'm right where God called me." Roger paused and looked at her. "Then why am I dragging?"

"Roger, look what you've been through," Jeanne said with urgency in her voice. "Just the funerals and hospital work alone — you've had so many lately."

Roger thought back, and he couldn't believe it himself. Since Tim had died, he'd had to lead some of the toughest funerals he'd ever had. One was for a man with eight kids, half of them at home. He died suddenly of a heart attack, leaving them all behind. Then there was a stillbirth. Not long after that, a college student came home for surgery because he'd been found to have testicular cancer. Then a two-year-old was struck with Wilm's Disease, cancer of the kidney. He had to have a kidney removed and begin chemotherapy. Not more than a few months after that, another college student had symptoms that were diagnosed as Hodgkin's disease. All of that in less than a year. The whole church was reeling.

"You're right, Jeanne," Roger finally said. "I hadn't thought through all that, but that's got to be working on me. I'm not the kind of guy who can keep from getting emotionally involved with my people. I've poured myself into every one of those situations."

The deacons' meetings had been tense for the past few months, with occasional criticisms of something Roger was doing, so he went into the April meeting with his guard up. The meeting went along smoothly until about halfway through, when Buck said, "Pastor, I have something I'd like to bring up that isn't on the agenda."

Roger looked over the rest of the agenda, and nothing couldn't wait if it had to. "Go ahead," he said, his stomach tensing.

"I have heard several complaints about your counseling, and they greatly concern me. In fact, I think they should concern all of us here."

"What exactly have you heard? It's hard for me to respond if I don't know the specifics."

"They say that you're counseling beyond your expertise. You string people along, don't really help them, but refuse to refer them to the help they need."

"Who's been saying that?" Roger wanted to know.

"Several people. I don't think it's fair for me to break a confidence to give you names."

"But several people have said that?"

Buck paused. Then he said, "Well, just one."

"Who is it?"

Buck crossed his big arms across his chest. "I can't say."

Roger suspected it was Marybeth, who by now was seeing a professional counselor. *Maybe she's finally getting help from him,* he thought, *and that's why she's carping at me.* He wanted to say her name, but as a pastoral counselor he felt an obligation to protect her and not get embroiled in the details of her case.

"If you're not willing to tell me who the person is, how can I responsibly defend myself?" Roger finally said.

"Well, that's not the only thing," Buck said.

By this time, Dominic was leaning forward and drumming his fingers on the table. "Roger, do you realize you've run twenty minutes over time on several Sundays?" he broke in.

"That's not true, Dom," Roger said.

"But it is!" Dominic's hands were moving rapidly.

"I watch the clock very carefully," Roger protested. "And I've got tapes of every message I've given. If you go back and listen to them, you'll see that I've never gone more than five minutes over. Ever."

Dom was quiet then, and Roger knew it was because he was flat wrong. But the whole accusation rankled Roger. A genuine charge he could understand, but this kind of petty, imaginary thing was beyond his comprehension. And why was he the only one to defend himself? He looked around at the other deacons, and he knew most of them supported him. Why wouldn't they speak up?

"If that's all, then we'll get back to the agenda," Roger said.

"While we're on preaching, I'd like to say something," said Matt, a young businessman who sometimes crossed the line between being assertive and aggressive. "Why don't you ever preach from the Gospel of John? That's a great book for new Christians, but all we hear is Ephesians, Ephesians, Ephesians."

"That's because right now I'm in a series on Ephesians. But I regularly return to the Gospels."

"Well, it's important for our church to get some of that basic material. First Peter would be good, too."

Roger didn't mind a suggestion, but he balked at letting a

brand-new Christian, which Matt was, set his entire preaching schedule. But he stayed calm. "I appreciate the suggestion," he managed.

Then Buck was back at it. "You know, Roger, you use Greek words a lot in your sermons, and I think that's just confusing to people. Nobody gets helped by that."

"I sometimes will refer to the original language to highlight a certain meaning in the text," Roger said, "but I don't think I do that overmuch. And several people have told me how helpful that is to them."

"The job of a preacher is to make the text plain," Buck instructed him.

Roger didn't know what to say that would make any difference.

When Roger drove home, at 11:30, he kept trying to think how he could explain how he felt to Jeanne. "I feel like I've been through a paper shredder," was what he finally settled on.

That Thursday, he came home from the church for dinner and sat down in the La-Z-Boy until Jeanne finished getting things ready. The next thing he knew, she was standing next to him, shaking his arm.

"Huh? Did I fall asleep?" Roger asked her groggily.

"Yes, Honey. Come to dinner."

After dinner, Jeanne said she had something she wanted to show him. She disappeared down the hall and came back in a few moments with a paperback book. "I've been reading a very interesting book about emotional depletion and discouragement and burnout," she said, "and I want to read you just a portion of it."

"C'mon, Honey. I'm okay."

"No, I just want to read you this short quiz. Please, do it for me."

"Okay."

Jeanne began reading the questions — "Do you find yourself forgetting what you were saying in the middle of a conversation?" "Do you wake up tired?" — and marked Roger's responses on a notepad. When they were all done, she tallied the results.

"How'd I do?" Roger was by this time intrigued.

"There are thirty points possible, and according to this, you're in danger if you score sixteen or more. And your score is . . ." She stopped her pencil. "Twenty-eight." She looked over at him. "Roger, I'm going to call the doctor right now."

"Now wait, Jeanne. That's just one little quiz."

"You just about hit the top! I have watched you, and you are not the same person. You come home tired; you snap at me over little things; you drag around like the most discouraged, blue person I've ever met. That's not right. Honey, I'm worried about you."

Roger stayed silent. He hated the thought of going to a doctor over this, but he knew she was right.

Jeanne left a message with the answering service, and in about a half hour the doctor called back. After hearing the symptoms, the doctor ordered some medication to get Roger's nerves calmed down and asked to see him the next day.

With the medication, Roger began to perk up. But when he was feeling good, he would set the pills aside, and then he'd take a nosedive again. The worst time of month was the night of the board meeting. He'd be tense for two days before. Business had basically ground to a halt; whatever Roger suggested, Buck and Dom fought, and usually they were able to persuade one or two people to their side. Without a lot of new programs to discuss, that left time to snipe at Roger. At the May meeting, Roger was amazed at how little things he'd done and said could be completely twisted and misunderstood until they looked bad. He was fighting hearsay, rumors, half-truths, and they seemed to be winning. Finally, he made an impassioned plea to the board: "Gentlemen, please, a lot of these things here are just the product of talking that has gotten out of hand and been greatly exaggerated. For the sake of the church, we've got to keep what is said here confidential." Then he decided to go for the face-off. "Dom, I heard this week, for example, that you have been talking to several people in the church about matters before this board."

Everyone turned and looked at Dom. "No way," he said. "I haven't said a word to anybody, and I resent the accusation."

"I heard that from a very reliable source, Dom." Roger held his ground.

"Well, they're wrong." Dom's eyes flashed. "If word's getting out, it's not through me."

After that meeting Roger thought for the first time, *I don't know how much longer I can take this.*

The very next day a woman from the church called him. "Pastor Landis, what's going on?"

"What do you mean?" Roger asked.

"Dominic Perra is doing some carpentry work at my house today, and ever since he's been here he's been complaining about this person and that person. Is there something going on with the church?" *I knew it,* Roger thought. *Everything I've said in deacons' meetings has gotten out and been twisted.*

Roger tried to assure her everything was under control and that people needed to be patient and prayerful while a few things worked themselves out.

If only I believed that, he thought as he hung up.

The June meeting was the worst yet. Buck and Dom rehashed complaints about using too many Greek words, counseling beyond his expertise, and others that Roger had already tried to explain. Then Buck looked at him and said, "You know, Pastor, we are really disappointed that you didn't handle your son's death right. We were looking for an example, and you didn't give us one."

Roger's mouth dropped open, and he stared. He finally closed his mouth again and remained silent for a while. He didn't know whether to try to explain, to lash back, or just cry. "Jeanne and I felt we handled it well. I mean, people said we did . . . " Then Roger trailed off and looked down.

The room got very quiet, and then Buck cleared his throat. "Well, let's move on to the next item of business."

Two nights later, as usual, Roger couldn't sleep. He kept

replaying Buck saying, "You didn't handle your son's death right." He thought about Tim. *Oh, if only you could see me now, Son,* he thought. *I wish you were here to help.* Roger tried to pray and clear his mind, but his thoughts kept drifting back to the deacons' meetings. In a few more weeks he was going to have to face another meeting, and it would probably be his last. He had heard Buck and Dom were pushing the other deacons to ask him to resign. He felt as if he were in a small, black room and the walls and floor and ceiling were all moving in on him. He got up and headed for the bathroom.

He switched on the light, put both palms on the sink counter, and leaned forward and looked at himself in the mirror. *If only I could get to sleep and just rest for a long time,* he thought. *I need to rest. I've got to get out of here somehow.* He reached up, swung back the mirror, and looked at his bottle of medication. *Thirty pills. That ought to do it.*

No, what would Jeanne do? She'd be crushed. Roger looked down, then back up at the bottle. *They'd go down easy.*

But then a picture of his daughter, Caroline, came to his mind. He straightened up and turned to go.

Then he turned around again and stood frozen, staring at the cabinet for a long time. *They'd never understand,* he finally thought. *They'd think Jesus let me down.*

He went back to bed. *Lord,* he prayed as he tried to fall asleep, *I just can't hack it anymore. I can't.*

Fortunately, Roger's story does not end there, and we'll pick up his story again in a later chapter. But his experience illustrates the painful fact that even skilled, veteran pastors can be shattered by discouragement.[1]

How can pastors overcome discouragement? How can they persevere through and beyond dark periods and continue an effective ministry? A Southern Baptist pastor wrote LEADERSHIP: "How can I live beyond, and be effective again after, disillusionment with people and the destruction of idealism? I've been betrayed and abandoned. How can I be restored to fellowship, to ministry?"

What are the secrets to staying power, to crossing the finish line after a lifetime of successful ministry? The rest of this book tackles that question.

---

1. Throughout the book I use the word *discouragement* to describe a broad range of common human emotions, such as frustration, hopelessness, and disappointment. I do not, however, mean it to refer to clinically discernible depression. Depression, while sharing some characteristics with discouragement, is more complex and does not necessarily respond to the same treatments (many of which are discussed in this book). For a helpful discussion of depression in the ministry, readers are referred to *Coping with Depression in the Ministry and Other Helping Professions* by Archibald D. Hart (Word, 1984).

T W O

OCCUPATIONAL HAZARDS

The occupational hazard of the Christian ministry and evangelism is discouragement.

JOHN R. W. STOTT

Those whom the Lord has destined for this great office he previously provides with the armor which is requisite for the discharge of it, that they may not come empty and unprepared.

JOHN CALVIN

For a year now I have been talking with pastors from across the country about the joys and the discouragements of their ministries. I have sat in the offices of dozens of these church leaders and read surveys from nearly two hundred more.

With some, I have been privileged to share in the high point of their ministries. "After ten years in ministry," wrote one, "my greatest sense of encouragement has come this year. I'm *enjoying* ministry." I've seen others in deep crevices: "I've never been so discouraged," said a minister in his forties. "This week I sent out twenty-two résumés."

What news can I report from the armloads of surveys and hours of tape?

A combination of good news and bad news.

First, the good news: Many, many pastors feel fulfilled in their calling and committed to their work. The vast majority of respondents to the LEADERSHIP survey said they feel positive about their ministry. Writes a Christian Church minister: "I've seen people changed by Jesus Christ. What else could I do with my life that would really count for something like that?"

The bad news: Thousands of pastors feel lonely, fatigued,

discouraged, and ready to quit. Nearly half of all pastors responding to the LEADERSHIP survey said they regularly or often feel discouraged about their ministry.

The Channel Swim

The English Channel, that twenty-one-mile stretch of water between Dover and Calais, is still the ultimate challenge in long-distance swimming. "Ask channel swimmers what makes it tough," writes Robert Glass, "and they invariably mention the cold. During the swimming season, the water is usually about 60 degrees. Nobody tries it without a thick coating of grease to hold in body warmth.

"Then there are the stinging jellyfish, the throat-parching salt water, floating logs, diesel fumes from the escort boat, winds that come from nowhere — a strong breeze can stir up swells twice a man's height — and the opposing tides down from the North Sea and up that channel that drag a swimmer into an S course and nearly always add ten miles or so.

"At least two people have died swimming the channel, and scores have been pulled out, exhausted and suffering from exposure."[1]

I thought of Glass's account recently as I read comments from pastors who have written to LEADERSHIP. "My number one struggle in the ministry is discouragement," wrote one pastor who is growing tired from the swim. One pastor who is suffering from exposure was blunt about it: "I'm in ministry only because I spent thousands of dollars preparing for it and I don't have training to do anything else. As soon as I can, I'm getting out."

"Discouragement is a big issue for the pastor," says Steve Harris, pastor of Maple Lake (Minnesota) Baptist Church. "You can be discouraged by your ministry, and if you don't do something with that, it can slide into discouragement with your life, with your marriage. Dealing with discouragement is a matter of life and death for me."

In short, ministry subjects a person to certain hazards.

Eugene Peterson, pastor of Christ Our King Presbyterian Church in Bel Air, Maryland, tells how he was at a Red Cross bloodmobile to donate his annual pint, and a nurse was asking him a series of questions to see if there was any reason for disqualification. "The final question on the list was 'Do you engage in hazardous work?' " Eugene remembers. "I said, 'Yes.' "[2]

What are these occupational hazards of the pastoral ministry, these floating logs that may catch many ministers by surprise? What factors are most likely to cause a pastor to be discouraged?

The Dirty Near-Dozen

The LEADERSHIP survey revealed a variety of discouraging factors, but pastors put these at the top of their list:

A sense of incompleteness, the feeling that nothing is ever finished, nothing is fully accomplished. Says Rick McKinniss, pastor of Kensington (Connecticut) Baptist Church, "The most discouraging aspect of being a pastor, I find, is the incompleteness of it all. Your product is people, and they are always in process." Because of that, a pastor can never go home at the end of the day and say, "Boy, that feels good. I finished everything I wanted to do today."

Another reason for the feeling, as a pastor of a small church points out, is that "I have so many irons in the fire, it's hard to concentrate on one and really see progress in any one area."

The rate of my church's growth. More pastors identified this as their greatest discourager than any other item. Writes a Christian Church minister on the West Coast: "In spite of ten years of hard work, there's been a lack of visible church growth in my present ministry." Down the road from him are churches that grew to several thousand at meteoric speed. No matter how many plausible sociological reasons there may be for the church's plateau, he feels a nagging sense of angst. "I think I'm doing a good job. I know I am. Then why aren't we growing?"

Lack of family time. Gary Downing, executive minister of Colonial Church of Edina, Minnesota, knows the struggle. "As recently as last night I missed dinner because of a couple in crisis who needed time and needed it now. Having to make that call home was so tough. You dial slowly because you know what the response is going to be on the other end, and you kind of wince when you hear it."

Apathetic volunteers. "It appeared for a few months that the vision was being caught by our elders to press ahead with a shepherding ministry and a building program," wrote one pastor on the LEADERSHIP survey. "But this was short-lived. Their slackness in doing the little things made me aware they could not handle anything bigger. To lead our folks further would only result in much more work for me personally. I just don't sense the needed support from the elders and deacons. They say, 'Yes, let's do it!' but then don't carry out their plans." Apathetic lay leaders have enervated this pastor's spirit. He admits he has given thought to leaving the pastoral ministry altogether.

My level of compensation. Like mononucleosis, low pay causes a persistent, draining sense of helplessness. As one pastor put it succinctly, "It is hard to serve when you're worrying about how the bills will be paid."

"A few vocal members" are the bane of countless pastors. Three deacons, two families, five committee members — a tiny coalition that harasses a pastor with gossip and criticism. Their numbers are few, but their impact is great. "We had nearly completed a vast building project," writes one pastor, "and some people in the church were negative about what I was doing. I focused more on these few personalities than on anything else. I became physically ill and entered a cycle of depression."

My diverse job expectations/roles. Gone are the days of the parson who merely preached, married, and buried. Today's pastor is expected to administrate, counsel, lead music, teach, write, intervene in conflict, visit, evangelize, and on and on. "I have thought of leaving pastoral ministry," admits a pastor, "and what has most led me to feel this way is that the expectations are virtually unreal."

Doing church administration. Many pastors went into the ministry because they wanted to preach, study, pray, and give spiritual guidance. Often they end up with papers at a desk. The administration ranges from the mundane (calling in orders for Sunday school curriculum, recruiting a third-grade teacher, and making sure the copier repairman shows up) to the mammoth (projecting and managing budgets that, even in the smaller church, may range in the hundreds of thousands of dollars). Phil Sackett, pastor of the Excelsior (Minnesota) Bible Church, admits, "Administration drains me because that's not where I feel I'm gifted. Doing something outside your gifted area is more a drain than working in line with your gifts."

Counseling. The final entry on the "Least Wanted" list may be something of a surprise. After all, counseling is at the heart of the ministerial role; it's direct work with people in a helping capacity. But many pastors said counseling wears them down. Part of the reason may be the increasing complexity of problems today. Another may be how quickly counseling can consume a minister's schedule. But the main reason may be the simple fact that dealing with troubled people drains you. As one pastor put it, "The church seems more and more the place where people dump their garbage, and the minister is frequently the primary dumping spot."

Inside Slide

The factors listed above are all external; they are part of the pastoral task and come at the pastor from the outside. Accompanying these are internal sources of discouragement, inner feelings and attitudes that may drag a church leader down.

"The pastorate isn't supposed to be this way." The pastor enters his or her work with a sense of divine realities. The work is filled with eternal import. He or she dreams of unity in the body of Christ, of spiritual growth.

Indeed, the pastoral task calls for that. As Gary McIntosh, formerly a pastor and now a seminary professor, writes: "Robert Schuller says the pastor ought to be hired to dream dreams and then execute them. Robert Dale adds in *To Dream Again*, 'Behind every great achievement is a dreamer of great dreams. Much more than a dreamer is required to bring it to reality; but the dream must be there first.' . . . Healthy churches have a dream of what God wants to do through them. And the pastor is the chief dreamer."

And yet there's a built-in liability: The person who dreams can be dashed when those dreams don't come to pass. To be successful a pastor must dream, but to do so is to invite disappointment.

Paired with this is the common clerical question, *Am I doing any good*? Pastors, who deal with matters of the spirit, have a tough time quantifying their work. Few clear bench marks exist. Says Robert Hudnut, pastor of First Presbyterian Church in Winnetka, Illinois: "I find that on some Saturday nights I'm asking, *Am I doing anything worthwhile? Have I made any difference in anybody's life? How many have turned the corner for Christ?* The other day I was talking with my mother about my job. She said, 'You're making a wonderful contribution with your life.' I want to believe that, but sometimes I wonder."

"I can't talk to anyone." Pastors listen to members' deepest problems — and must keep the information confidential. Ben Haden, pastor of Chattanooga, Tennessee's, First Presbyterian Church, says, "So much of what you know, you cannot share with anyone else without breaching confidence, and nothing destroys ministry more quickly than running off at the mouth."

Even basic concerns about the church or worries about the ministry can't be shared with members of the congregation for fear they will create ripples of unrest.

Related to this is the feeling expressed by Steve Harris: "Nobody outside the pastorate *really* understands what it's like."

"Every day I am under the pressure of my concern for all the churches," was the way the apostle Paul described a final inner difficulty for the church leader. "When someone is weak, then I feel weak too; when someone is led into sin, I am filled with distress" (2 Cor. 11:28–29, GNB). A parent feels pain when a six-year-old daughter falls off her bike and has to be rushed to the emergency room. In the same way, a pastor, charged with the spiritual care of many people, feels pain when any one of them falls into sin, is sick, or gets hurt.

Resources

Though it's essential to understand what causes discouragement, we must keep in mind the joys and the encouragements of ministry, the substantial and overwhelming resources on the pastor's side. Caleb and Joshua, the two spies who brought a positive report on the Land, recognized honestly the giants they faced but remembered as well, "We are strong enough to conquer."

One survey response that impressed me was from a minister in his fifties who reflected on his current pastorate, a situation of immense pain. "Church morale has seemed to drop," he wrote, "and people have been leaving. Attendance is on the decline, for a number of reasons. The community has been hit by a serious economic crunch, causing many to move away. Then I had to deal with a couple of discipline problems in the church, and even though the church lay leaders were also involved, the burden for those people leaving was placed on me. I've had just about all I can take."

But this minister is not giving up. He's not looking to leave the ministry. Part of the reason, he says, is his "sense that this is what God has called me to do." But in addition, he has been able to remember the blessed encouragers that are also the minister's portion. He has kept a hopeful eye on them. As he puts it, "I still have the realization that when circumstances are right, I can't imagine anything I would enjoy doing more."

What are these encouragements in ministry, the oases that

THREE

OCCUPATIONAL HIGHLIGHTS

I knew an old minister once. . . . How I envy him. . . . I am listed as a famous home-runner, yet beside that obscure minister, who was so good and so wise, I never got to first base!

BABE RUTH

Blessed are the presbyters who have gone before in the way, who came to a fruitful and perfect end; for they need have no fear lest anyone depose them from their assigned place.

CLEMENT OF ROME

Thee discouragements in ministry are not the whole story, as even the most battered and weary pastor will attest. In fact, often in the very midst of the doldrums comes the sudden gust of hope.

"I had a terrible death last week in our congregation," relates Eugene Peterson, pastor of Christ Our King Presbyterian Church in Bel Air, Maryland. "A woman was killed in an automobile accident, and she was only fifty years old. She was such a lively person, so full of life. And the accident was terrible. Five women were traveling together in a van when a big truck plowed into them, and all five were killed.

"The accident happened in the afternoon, but her husband didn't find out about it until seven or eight o'clock at night. I got a call at nine. As I got in the car and began driving to their house, about three miles down the road, I thought about Bill, and how much he loved her, and about the three kids, all in college. I knew how devastating this would be to them, and I just didn't think I could face that. This was the fourth death in our congregation in just two months, and all of them were unnatural — interrupted lives. I thought, *Lord, I can't do this. I don't want to be a pastor anymore. I just can't enter into that deep pain again. Or if I can, I don't want to. I just don't want to do this anymore.*

"So I got there," Eugene continues, "and two hours later I was coming back down the same road and I was praying, *Lord, I'm glad I'm a pastor. There's nothing I'd rather do than this. I'm just glad I'm a pastor. Thank you for letting me be a pastor.*"

The Most-Wanted List

When someone thanks God for being a pastor, what specific things can he or she be grateful for?

The LEADERSHIP survey asked church leaders to identify these and rank them. Each one that made the list is a powerful encourager, a resource for staying power.

Topping the list by an overwhelming margin were *my spouse* and *my family*. Steve Harris expresses the feelings of many pastors: "I can't imagine not having my wife's support. Pam hears what are, I'm sure, some terrible sermons in the beginning stages. But on Sunday she always has her notebook open and is eager to hear what I'm going to say. When we get home on Sunday, we can have good discussions about the sermon, because she's not somebody who's going to say, 'Boy, that was great' when it wasn't. But she's going to be there and point out what was good and helpful. That's a great source of strength to me. I guess I wouldn't be in ministry today if it weren't for her support."

Adds another pastor: "When you come home to a kid jumping up and down in the doorway because Daddy's home — it's hard to get any more encouraging than that."

Two other highly rated sources of encouragement were *sermon preparation* and *delivery* (the related *leading worship* also garnered high marks). Explains the pastor of a church in the Midwest: "There's something in the discipline of preparing for preaching that is completely mysterious; it lifts you. There have been times when I've been so low that I felt I *had* to write a sermon. And when I did, I felt on top of the world again." Though study is strenuous, as a pastor meditates on God's

Word, he or she becomes refreshed, "like a tree planted by streams of water."

Delivering the sermon is another high point. Says the same pastor: "I feel more alive, more present with the people when I'm preaching than at any other time. That's when I really feel in touch with them, so in some ways I'd rather be there than anywhere else."

A third encourager was *vacations,* no surprise, and *rest/relaxation/exercise* was also named frequently. Edward Bratcher, pastor of the Manassas (Virginia) Baptist Church, says, "Stress interruption is essential. If you can get away, you can get a clear picture of where you are and find a new sense of hope."

Being friends with members of our church was named a boost by many. Harley Schmitt, pastor of Brooklyn Park Lutheran Church in suburban Minneapolis, says, "People in the body are a real source of encouragement. In fact, I think they are one of the three basic encouragers: the Word, prayer, and God's people.

"Recently we've been making some critical, long-range decisions as a church, and those are difficult. We had a congregational meeting last Sunday, and I shared how I felt, how hard some of the decisions were for me, too. Later in the week, a member brought some flowers from the family garden and said, 'I just want you to know, Harley, that my husband and I are thinking of you.' As I've sat at my desk this week, I've looked at these beautiful flowers, and they keep reminding me that somebody cared enough to say, 'We sense this time is hard for you, too.' Things like this are a big source of encouragement."

A related encourager that placed high was *friends outside the church.* As one pastor explained, "It's great having friends outside the church; you can talk freely with them about the ministry because they are not in it."

Visitation is a shot in the arm for most pastors because it's an opportunity to give direct, immediate help to a person in need. Ben Haden, pastor of First Presbyterian Church in

Chattanooga, admits, "When I'm discouraged, the first thing I do as personal therapy is visit people in the hospital. I've never gone to the hospital and not come away encouraged. It's gotten to the point now that if my wife detects I'm discouraged, she says, 'Ben, why don't you go to the hospital?' "

A good relationship with leaders, whether staff or the board, is another source of refreshment. When leaders support their pastor and work with him or her, they give the pastor staying power. Writes a Texas pastor: "In all my ministry, I've never experienced a greater sense of encouragement than one night recently when a group of our deacons made a commitment to meet weekly and pray for God's blessing on my ministry."

These factors are great encouragers, but they're still not the greatest. Most pastors went on to list two more. Together, they may be the ultimate weapon in the battle against discouragement.

Two Eternal Realities

God's call. "I believe I was called by God, and that's enough for me," wrote one pastor.

"I want to stay in ministry because I've answered Christ's call to love him by preaching, teaching, and loving his people," wrote another.

A sense of divine call is the great slab of bedrock upon which ministry rests. This sense, though interpreted differently by pastors, is the solid, deeply buried conviction that withstands the quakes of discouragement. It's what maintained Isaiah and gave Jeremiah courage, and it's what gives perseverance to pastors today. "A pastor will have to graciously put up with people who are self-centered, thoughtless, and cranky at times," wrote one person, "so he must know God has placed him there."

One pastor who left the ministry couldn't get rid of that sense of call. "I fought that idea," he writes, "and I left the ministry for a year and a half. But inside me there was this growing conviction that the ministry is the place God wants me. So now I'm pastoring again."

A New England pastor wanted to leave the ministry and had several solid job leads. But he decided to stay in the pastorate, and now he's enjoying ministry again. He says, "Through my difficult time at the church, and while I was looking for ways to get out, I learned something: If God calls you to ministry, he will keep you going. He's ultimately responsible for that."

Philip Hinerman is a good example. He has served as pastor of Park Avenue United Methodist Church in Minneapolis for the last thirty-six years, and during the first twenty-six years literally thousands of members pulled out, angry, as the neighborhood changed and the congregation became integrated. How did he survive the years of turmoil? "I am not particularly strong physically," he admits, "and I am not particularly strong where critics are concerned. I feel a lot of pain from my critics. And I'm not great at confrontation — and yet I've had a whole lifetime of confrontation to face. If I were doing this in the flesh, I would have run out of steam thirty-five years ago. I know I'm not the kind of person who could have endured this.

"But every morning since I was fifteen years old," he continues, "I've gotten up and surrendered my life to Christ. Those hours of prayer and Bible study every morning are what save me."

In this way, Phil Hinerman and countless pastors past and present have renewed their sense of call.

God's changing lives through your ministry. A second foundation stone, touching the first, is captured by Gary Downing: "The thing that is most inspiring and encouraging — the kind of thing you want to jump up and click your heels and shout 'Hurrah!' about — is to be able to participate in the process of a person meeting the Lord.

"This year I sat with some young guys who were at a fork in the road in their lives. They knew they needed to make a decision. We talked together, and then I prayed with them as they haltingly invited Christ to come and be their friend. There's nothing like that. It's an awe-inspiring peek into eternity.

"When you see God's Spirit move in another person's life, it also reconfirms what God has done in your own life. Suddenly those early morning breakfast meetings begin to make sense and be worth rolling out of bed for. It says it's all worthwhile."

Particularly satisfying is the knowledge that such labor yields eternal results. Says Delbert Rossin, pastor of Faith Lutheran Church in Geneva, Illinois: "If you build a car, as great an achievement as that is, it rusts out in ten or twenty years. But if you help someone build a Christian life, the results of your work last for eternity."

Writes a pastor on the LEADERSHIP survey: "Shortly after I came to my present church I began working with a man who was near bottom in alcoholism. His wife and teenage son were also drug abusers.

"But today, after working with them over a three-year period, the family is sober. The man is working as a counselor in a drug-treatment facility. The wife completed nursing school and is working as a nurse. And the son is succeeding in school.

"I am encouraged today in that I know *for sure* God's love works miracles. I've seen those miracles."

Pastors who've seen miracles are able to see through the stretches, even long ones, of discouragement.

Five Cries

Chapters 2 and 3 have quickly scanned the ups and downs of ministry. But it's intriguing to take a closer look at the list of pastoral discouragers. The first thing you notice is that certain ones cluster together.

After a little sorting of the list of discouragers, you can hear five major "cries":
- I'm not able to see any progress.
- I'm not able to do what I'm really gifted to do.
- I'm facing a few difficult members who are causing me pain.

- I'm not getting affirmation for what I do.
- I'm not able to get enough rest and relaxation.

These haunting cries come from deep within. If they go unheeded, the pastor feels abandoned, frustrated, and ultimately, discouraged.

But those same cries can also be transformed into shouts of joy. The next chapters explore how.

Part II
CRIES

F O U R

I CAN'T SEE ANY PROGRESS

*I believe God wants us to be successful
. . . and yet success is not always
obvious. The Chinese bamboo tree does
absolutely nothing — or so it seems —
for the first four years. Then suddenly,
sometime during the fifth year, it shoots
up ninety feet in sixty days. Would you
say that bamboo tree grew in six weeks,
or five years?*

*I think our lives are akin to the
Chinese bamboo tree. Sometimes we put
forth effort, put forth effort, and put forth
effort . . . and nothing seems to happen.
But if you do the right things long
enough, you'll receive the rewards of
your efforts.*

S. TRUETT CATHY

Imagine the elation of architect Robert Mills. On that day in 1836, the fledgling Washington National Monument Society announced they had chosen *his* plans for the soon-to-be-constructed monument to the nation's first president. Mills had slaved for months over the elaborate drawings, and he had dared to dream big — a granite obelisk soaring over 555 feet high. It would be no less than the tallest structure in the world. Mills had designed many other buildings in his career, but this monument was different. And now his dreams were becoming reality.

But the funds didn't come in as fast as the society had hoped. Construction wasn't able to begin for five years, ten years — a full twelve years later. Then the engineers discovered the ground at the site was too soft to support the weight of the huge monument, so they had to start over farther north. Work proceeded fairly smoothly for six years, and major figures began donating marble to the project. But in 1854, when Pope Pius IX donated a marble block from the Temple of Concord, a group of saboteurs stole the block and destroyed it. The incident shocked the public, and donations nearly stopped. Then members of the Know-Nothing political party broke into the society's offices and actually seized possession of the monument. Vandals continued to deface the monument, and construction finally stopped dead in 1855.

What remained of Mills's soaring dream was a squat, ugly 150-foot stump. When Robert Mills died that year, he must have died with a broken heart.[1]

When I read about Mills's profound disappointment — the slow, fitful progress; the interruptions; the harassing circumstances; the glorious dream begging for fulfillment — I was struck by how similar his feelings were to those of some pastors.

One Presbyterian minister recalls his days in a congregation in New Jersey. "I loved that church, and I poured myself into it. The church really needed to turn around, and I began to see signs of that. New people began to come. In about five years, 40 percent of the church was new people.

"But trying to get anything done was next to impossible. Convincing the Session to try something new was hard enough, but then the trustees would have to allocate the funds for it. And the trustees and the Session could never seem to agree.

"I had a couple who were marvelous youth group leaders. They were young, they had great hearts, and they were really doing something with the kids. But everything they tried to do was blocked. The church owned a house that the couple wanted to use for the kids. It would have been great, and I pushed for it, but the trustees kept dragging their feet. It finally came down to a fire extinguisher — the trustees wouldn't finance a fire extinguisher they needed to meet the code. The couple gave up and quit leading the youth group.

"After a few battles like that, I realized I wasn't going to change things any time soon. It was going to take at least ten years, and by that time I would have died. So I left."

No change. No growth. No progress. Nothing moving ahead that says, "You're doing a good job." Situations like this dog some pastors. They can't shake the feeling that all their work and dreams will never move beyond the awkward,

150-foot stump of their present situation.

The LEADERSHIP survey revealed three major factors that lead pastors to cry out, "I can't see any progress!" They vary in intensity and difficulty, but each in its own way hinders the mission ministers long to complete and leads to discouragement:

- constant interruptions
- lethargic church boards
- slow church growth.

Progress Buster #1: Interruptions

Interruptions, ranked as the number one source of discouragement on the LEADERSHIP survey, arise because pastors are on emergency call twenty-four hours a day. Those calls, coming unexpected as they do, quickly add stress. Ministers who had hoped to limit their week to a manageable number of hours suddenly find themselves adding on the draining work of comforting a grieving widow, or sitting with a family in a hospital waiting for test results. Meanwhile, important work such as writing Sunday's sermon must be dropped, perhaps not to be picked up again until late Saturday night.

The calls of urgent need, though, are readily accepted, even gloried in, by most pastors. Explains Ed Bratcher: "I have never felt comfortable with not being able to be reached. My secretaries do try to guard my study time, but to me there is something in the role of a pastor that says the pastor should be available. When you think about it, the pastor is the one person in our society who is still readily available to people. If hurting people call up their counselor or psychiatrist, they get an appointment a week later or three weeks later. If they call their physician they may not be able to get in for several days. So when they need me as their pastor, I want to be there."

When genuinely hurting people call, pastors know they were ordained "for such a time as this" and move with compassion.

"A man in our congregation, a sweet Southern-gentleman

kind of guy about seventy years old, came down with a brain tumor about two weeks ago and died within a week," said Steve Harris. "To be in that little room with his wife and their kids when they found out, and to have them later say 'Thank you for being there,' —that's when I sense I'm doing what God put me here for."

The more frustrating interruptions are of another class. The florist calls to find out how early the church will be open on Saturday so she can set up for the wedding. The volunteer in the food pantry wants to know what happened to the food request forms they've been using. And there's a constant flow of people who stop by "just to talk." A recent LEADERSHIP cartoon depicted a pastor praying on his knees in his office. In the doorway stand three women saying, "We don't know what you've been doing in here, Pastor, but we've been waiting five minutes to tell you there's a broken hand dryer in the ladies' room."

Interruptions like these led time-management expert Ed Dayton to conclude, "If you're a pastor, never plan on doing an hour's work in an hour."

Interrupting the Interruptions

How have church leaders come to grips with the unexpected ring of the phone and the unplanned-for knock on the door? Here are the adjustments, both internal and external, ministers have made to stop — or at least interrupt — their interruptions.

Plan for emergencies. That sounds like double-talk, but it reflects an idea clergy have found helpful: accept that emergency situations are a part of pastoral life, and build flex time into the schedule accordingly. Lem Tucker, president of Voice of Calvary in Jackson, Mississippi, is one leader who has reached that point of acceptance. "I'm becoming more and more convinced," he writes, "that God's leader will never be allowed to get too comfortable. There will always be something coming undone, one more thing careening out of control." That reality led an East Coast pastor to "try to have some built-in time for emergencies. If I feel I need eight more hours of study in a particular week, I try to bracket ten to twelve hours for it. It helps me deal with the unexpected."

Bunch related tasks. This doesn't lower the number of interruptions, but it does make the uninterrupted hours far more productive. Don Gerig, a pastor for many years and now president of Fort Wayne (Indiana) Bible College, wrote in LEADERSHIP: "A friend involved in research told me his day is a success if he can spend two or three hours of solid, concentrated time on research. He knew there would be plenty of odds and ends to fill up the rest of the day.

"At first I thought he sounded lazy. The more I thought about it, looking at my own schedule, the more I understood. I had to ask myself, *How many times do I seriously devote even two uninterrupted hours a day to my important projects?"*

The "bunching" varies by preference, but many pastors have found it effective. One pastor does nothing but return and take calls during several two-hour blocks during his week. Another even skips meals so he does nothing on Tuesday and Wednesday but study, and then he's finished for the week. A third reserves all his mornings for prayer and study.

When interruptions do come, sort the major from the minor. At the instant of the call, though, when a person is distraught, that isn't easy. A Midwest pastor remembers: "One lady came to the door and wanted to pray about this friend who was seriously ill. I invited her in, and she told me how the friend had been hit by a car or something and was in the hospital. So we bowed our heads and I prayed for her friend. The lady left much relieved. I found out later she was talking about her pet rabbit."

As his story reminds us, not every situation demands a five-alarm response. Many could wait until later in the day or later in the week. Leith Anderson, pastor of Wooddale Church in Eden Prairie, Minnesota, explains: "At seminary a counseling professor told us, 'Anything that absolutely must be handled now — you're not capable of handling anyway.' That eliminates most emergencies. However, many of us in helping professions are driven primarily by a need for affirmation, and so we accommodate ourselves to everybody. That leads to burnout."

Adds an East Coast pastor who is now on the mission field, "I found that when I started asking people who 'had to see me right now' if they could wait a week, very often an interesting thing would happen. They would come into my office and say, 'Pastor, you know when I couldn't see you last week, I was really upset. But since I couldn't, I just kept crying out to the Lord about my problem, and he has given me a new peace about it. In fact, I feel like I've been able to forgive this person about the thing.' In many cases, because the people had to wait, they began to work out some of the problem themselves."

Progress Buster #2: Lethargic Church Boards

The second thing that blocks pastors from seeing any progress is more intense and more difficult to deal with, as a Southern pastor we'll call Keith found out.

"When I first came to the church," Keith recalls, "it was in a state of gridlock. As close as I could determine, no decision had been made in the church for several years. I quickly found out why.

"The committee on committees appointed the nominating committee. But the nominating committee selected the committee on committees. Some five people rotated back and forth every year between the two and thus were able to control everything that happened in the church. Plus, they had set it up so their friends who were officers in the church, like the Sunday school superintendent, were full-fledged voting members of every single committee. So five or ten people were stopping three hundred from doing anything.

"For the first six months I was here, there were only three items on the agenda of a committee, no matter which committee it was: who was going to paint the church sign in front, how we were going to get rid of the pigeons on the front porch, and when we were going to start using purchase orders. But they didn't want to decide anything about these issues; they just liked to get the discussion started and sit back and listen."

Though this may be an extreme case, you don't need to have a convoluted board structure to see progress blocked. It just depends on the people on the board. "The greatest time of discouragement in my ministry came at a finance committee meeting," wrote one pastor on the LEADERSHIP survey. "The men there objected to our giving scholarships of $20 per child for church camp that summer. Their rationale was 'No one ever gave us anything' and 'People don't need the money but will take it if it's given.' By contrast this group of men would have spared no expense on the maintenance of the building they had built. As a result of that decision, the CE director, who was the best we'd ever had, decided to resign. And we had no kids at camp that year.

"I am in the process of leaving," he continued. "I have led them as far as I can."

Probably no one has described the spirit of boards like these better than Chuck Swindoll. In *The Quest for Character* he writes of a fellow pastor who had encountered "the wrath of Khan" for trying something innovative. "Any leadership position, including ministry's, has its occupational hazards. But there are a few tests that can be endured only so long. One of them is *rigidity*.

"I don't know a better word for it. It's tough enough to deal with folks who choose to live that way themselves, but when they require it of us, ultimately restricting our vision for ministry, it becomes unbearable. Perhaps it is the closest we get to feeling suffocated."[2]

Quiet Consolation

You can expect pain — intense — in such a situation. Robert Boyd Munger, author of *My Heart — Christ's Home*, knew the difficulty as a young Presbyterian pastor. "When you try to change people who have never really known wholehearted commitment to Christ, and the old leadership is threatened by the younger eager beavers, you have tensions. I didn't know how to handle them then, and I was too proud to let anybody know what I was going through. I just redoubled my efforts to pray and work. But the pain was acute and it lasted a year and a half. There were times when I would have welcomed anything to get me out of that situation — even death. It was intolerable. How can you stand, still believing the gospel, still convinced that Christ is Lord, and yet you do not experience the reality of his warm, living presence? When there's nothing around that gives evidence of new life, when you see things falling apart — trouble with the choir, trouble with the youth?"

I asked Munger's questions of pastors. They offered no quick technique but the quiet consolation that comes from being there. Here are some of their reflections.

Try to give things time was a lesson many had learned. One couple found this, on a smaller scale, after working with what they called a "brick-wall youth group." Almost nothing positive happened for two years. But then in a few months they had more good conversations with kids than they'd had in the first twenty-two.

"When I'm tempted to get discouraged about progress with the board," says one pastor, "I like to think about Jesus' parable of the growing seed in Mark 4:26-29. First you have the seed, then it sprouts, then the stalk comes up, then the kernel sets on, and finally it becomes ripe. That has helped me realize that progress comes slowly, and even if all I've got right now is a little seed, it will keep growing."

Keith, the pastor who encountered a board logjam, found help in *trying to remove the key logs*. "One lady in particular would throw an awful scene, act ugly, so people would say, 'We don't want to upset Clair, so let her have her way.' So I resolved I would talk to her about it if it continued. So far, though, I haven't had to."

Keith also worked over a year or two to shift the board and committee structure to make it more difficult for people to hold voting positions indefinitely. That further isolated the ruling few, and today, he says, things are going fairly well.

Talking to someone outside the situation to keep perspective also helped Keith. A sluggish group of people makes you feel like Butch Cassidy when he said to the Sundance Kid, "I have vision, and the rest of the world wears bifocals." Someone from outside can keep that vision clear. When you're tempted to put on "bifocals" just to survive, when you begin to doubt your capability as a minister, it's time to talk with a friend. "I have a rather large long-distance phone bill," Keith admits.

Their final words of counsel can be summed up by the words of Corrie ten Boom: "No matter how deep our darkness, He is deeper still."

Progress Buster #3: Slow Church Growth

I love the early chapters of Acts, partly because there's so much going on. Evangelism, conversions, healing — it's exciting to see the fledgling church growing. You can feel the strong pulse in verses like Acts 6:7: "So the Word of God spread. The number of disciples in Jerusalem increased rapidly." Or Acts 9:31: "Then the church . . . enjoyed a time of peace. It was strengthened; and encouraged by the Holy Spirit, it grew in numbers, living in the fear of the Lord." Who wouldn't want to experience that kind of energy and growth in a church?

Thankfully, many pastors do. Others, however, don't. Nearly half of the pastors responding to the LEADERSHIP survey said "the rate of our church's growth" discourages them.

Few visitors, no conversions, a trickle of new members if any — it doesn't take much of that before you question what you're doing. Confesses a Christian Church minister who has seen little growth in his congregation: "I'm discouraged. I ask myself, *If we're doing things right, why aren't we growing?*"

Slow growth, perhaps more than anything else, erodes a pastor's self-esteem. Kent Hughes, now pastor of College Church in Wheaton, Illinois, writes of his experience trying to plant a church in California. "We had everything going for us. We had the prayers and predictions of our friends who believed a vast, growing work was inevitable. We had the sophisticated insights of the science of church growth. We had prime property in a fast-growing community. We had a superb nucleus of believers. And we had *me*, a young pastor with a good track record who was entering his prime.

"But to our astonishment and resounding disappointment, we didn't grow. In fact, by the middle of our second year, we typically counted fewer than half the regular attenders we had in the beginning. Our church was shrinking, and the prospects looked bad. *This can't be,* I thought. *I'm not living up to my expectations. I'm failing!"*

What makes the weekly attendance such a powerful influence on pastoral self-esteem? What gives the numbers their sting?

For one thing, "as pastors, we count the sheep," says a Lutheran minister. "That's a good and natural tendency. I think Jesus did that, and if we are to be shepherds, we need to be aware of individuals as well." No matter how large or small the church, there's a sense of care for each member. So when a member leaves, it hurts.

Surgeons have found that when a limb is amputated, the patient almost always sinks into depression. The same is true in the body of Christ: when a member is missing, the rest of the body, and particularly the pastor, feels it. In the words of a Presbyterian pastor: "It's hard to recognize that some people will leave. That must always be discouraging, because the Lord said, 'None have I lost.' "

The second factor is that pastoral work is with people and of a spiritual nature, so it's not easy to measure progress. As a result, the few physical factors — what one pastor calls "body, buck, and brick" — receive extra, and often undue, attention. "Look at the speakers and leaders for any ministerial gathering or church conference," says a pastor frustrated over his church's lack of growth. "The speaker is always someone who is 'minister of the 4,000-member First Church, which six months ago had twenty members.' You begin to wonder what's wrong with you, even if nothing is said outright."

Too, there's a self-defeating rule of thumb at work, a Methodist pastor points out: Decline is more discouraging, proportionately, than growth is encouraging. "When there's growth, I say, 'The Lord added this.' But when there's decline, I say, 'What am I doing wrong?' I blame myself." As a result, as one pastor said, "I don't know about other people, but for me it's always a struggle between a sense of failure and success."

Neutralizing the Numbers

Most of the adjustments pastors have made to lessen the discouraging effect of sluggish attendance figures are internal. Truly changing our approach toward something so closely tied to self-esteem takes time.

"I've finally come to the place now," one pastor told me, "where I realize that if I am a faithful preacher of the gospel, that's enough. Faithful is the only thing God ever asked us to be."

"How long did it take you to get to that point?" I asked him.

"As long as I've been preaching — about forty years."

There are, of course, external measures that can boost attendance, but increased size does not guarantee a freedom from the ongoing comparisons. One pastor I know leads a vital, multi-staff church of three hundred. He would be the envy of many smaller-church pastors, but he doesn't feel that. Instead he looks at the churches of five hundred and one thousand that are nearby and questions what he's doing wrong. Freedom comes not from size, which is a relative and shifting measure, but from an internal sense of worth based on entirely different criteria.

Here are some of the ways pastors have fine-tuned their thinking about growth over the years to lessen their discouragement.

The first several focus on the word *acceptance*. A Baptist pastor found freedom when he came to accept his church at the size it was. "I used to be bothered a lot when attendance was down. I remember one Sunday night coming into a sanctuary that holds two hundred and seeing three people. That's a real downer, especially if you think the others are staying away from you.

"But one thing that helped me," he continues, "was hearing Garrison Keillor on 'Prairie Home Companion.' He was talking about a small town, and he said its motto was 'We are what we are.' That phrase stuck with me as I came to this church. I decided I was going to love what we were. Not that we don't want to grow, but on a Sunday morning when the people gather, we are what we are. And I can accept that.

"I'm not saying I've fully conquered my feelings about size. But early in my ministry I'd look out and see the empty pews. Now I'm looking at the people who are there and trying to say something for them."

Accepting your current situation, no matter how limiting, as a call from God, is another lift. But oh, how difficult that is! Martin Luther, that towering giant of the Reformation, once confessed, "Next to faith this is the highest art — to be content with the calling in which God has placed you. I have not learned it yet." Maybe one reason it's so hard is that we consider how much more useful we could be in a larger setting. But that line of reasoning leads to despair. Then it's time to remember the stinging yet ultimately helpful words of Oswald Chambers: "Notice God's unutterable waste of saints, according to the judgment of the world. God plants His saints in the most useless places. We say, 'God intends me to be here because I am so useful.' Jesus never estimated His life along the line of the greatest use. God puts His saints where they will glorify Him, and we are no judges at all of where that is."[3]

A third road to acceptance is expressed by Phil Sackett of the Excelsior (Minnesota) Bible Church: "I had to learn to view the church not as my church but as the Lord's church. As long as I felt responsible for it — that how it progressed reflected on me and that I had to make it go — I lost a lot of energy. I had to come to the point of saying, 'It's his church, and if he doesn't want it to grow the way I would like it to, I'm willing for him to use it as it is.' I had to detach myself from the church enough that its ups and downs didn't totally sap my resources. That was a turning point for me."

A realization that has strengthened Steve Harris is that the life issues people face in a small church are just as difficult and significant as the issues in a larger church. The importance of the struggles and need for pastoral ministry are no less great. "Some people in Maple Lake Baptist Church, just a teeny country church on the side of Highway 55, are struggling right now with their marriages," he says. "One woman's husband is dying of cancer. A young guy is struggling with whether to go to seminary. A girl who just graduated from high school has been wondering *What am I going to do with my life?* Those are significant issues; they can't get any bigger. And what God says through me to these people is a gift."

In addition, some clergy have embraced the *benefits* of their smaller size. "I'm not sure I would be able to be a pastor of a 'superchurch,' " one says. "I gain encouragement from dealing with people on a one-to-one basis, where you can really have a spiritual conversation and deal with people's needs. And I probably wouldn't be able to do as much of that." Adds another pastor, "When you have nothing, you have nothing to lose. So you can become quite bold and you can take risks."

Others have tried to find different yardsticks for their ministry, ones that are more in keeping with the pastorate's fundamental nature. Since a pastor is called to "equip the saints," some look not to the number of saints but to the number equipped. "I was a fair-haired youth worker who had hundreds of kids coming to meetings," remembers one pastor. "But looking back, if I had to gauge my success, it wouldn't be by the number who came, but the number whom I nurtured to become Christian leaders. I can think of six people who are still ministering today, helping what's now a third and fourth generation of kids. That's what makes me feel good."

Ultimately, though, pastors in smaller situations find encouragement because they see God at work, even when that's barely discernible. It's that vision, the ability to see the

Spirit of God brooding over a church, that brings staying power. Oswald Chambers knew that when he wrote: "The test of a man's religious life and character is not what he does in the exceptional moments of life, but what he does in the ordinary times, when there is nothing tremendous or exciting on. . . . Don't give in because the pain is bad just now; get on with it, and before long you will find you have a new vision and a new purpose."[4]

Visions may sound flimsy, but when they're "engendered by the Scripture and supported by the Spirit" as one pastor put it, they sustain, they push through obstacles, they overcome.

There's a picture of that in the rest of the story of Robert Mills's vision, the Washington Monument. From the year Mills died, no work was done on the Washington Monument for a long twenty-five years. But somehow the dream Mills had had almost fifty years earlier wouldn't die. In 1880, with funds appropriated by Congress, work resumed, and four years later a cast-aluminum cap was placed over the granite tip. Today Mills's monument stands as the tallest masonry structure in the world.

Last year, over a million people came to see the realization of his dream.

1. Ron Schick, "Monumental America," *Modern Maturity* (August–September 1986), 54–55.
2. Charles R. Swindoll, *The Quest for Character* (Portland, Ore.: Multnomah, 1987).
3. Oswald Chambers, *My Utmost for His Highest* (New York: Dodd, Mead & Company, 1935), 223.
4. Ibid., 286.

FIVE

I'M NOT ABLE TO USE MY GIFTS

How do I maintain a sense of pastoral vocation in a community of people who hire me to do religious jobs?

EUGENE H. PETERSON

Ｏne of the worst years I ever had was in the early days of this church," recalls Eugene Peterson. "I realized I wasn't being a pastor. I was so locked into running the church program I didn't have time to be a pastor.

"The precipitating event was when one of my kids said, 'You haven't spent an evening at home for thirty-two days.' She had kept track! I was obsessive and compulsive about my administrative duties, and I didn't see any way to get out of the pressures that were making me that way. So I went to the Session one night and said, 'I quit.'

" 'I'm out all the time; I'm never at home,' I said. 'I'm doing all this administrative work, serving on all these committees, and running all these errands. I want to preach; I want to lead the worship; I want to spend time with people in their homes. That's what I came here to do. I want to be your spiritual leader; I don't want to run your church.' "

Not doing what I came here to do was not one of the potentially discouraging items listed on the LEADERSHIP survey, but it mounted an impressive write-in campaign. Pastor after pastor wrote of not being able to concentrate on the spiritual work he or she was gifted in and felt called to do —preaching and teaching, studying and praying, listening and offering guidance. They went into the ministry because they felt called to use these gifts and felt fulfilled when they did.

But somehow, after a few years in a church, they found to their dismay that they were spending large chunks of their time shuffling papers, putting out fires, administrating an organization. Illustrator Larry Thomas captured the feeling in an early LEADERSHIP cartoon in which a pastor sits at his kitchen table, head in hands. His wife says to him, "Today you've chaired three committee meetings, attended two potluck dinners, opened the bazaar, and refereed a boys' basketball game. How could you feel 'unfulfilled'?"

About thirty years ago Samuel Blizzard studied how Protestant ministers spent their time and how they felt about it. He reached a startling conclusion, writes Gaylord Noyce: "Ministers spent the most time at the job they liked least — administration; church management took almost 40 percent of their time. By contrast, the two activities that ministers liked doing the most, preaching and priestly leadership, together occupied only 20 percent of their time."[1]

Throwing yourself into your work and then realizing it isn't the work you want to be doing is a jump into chilly water. Glen Parkinson, pastor of Severna Park (Maryland) Presbyterian Church, remembers that realization hitting him during a previous pastorate. "I was just plugging away at my duties and I needed some kind of mental challenge, so I enrolled in the doctoral program at Westminster Seminary. As part of the entrance requirements, I had to write a paper on my philosophy of ministry, what I thought the ministry should be.

"So I wrote the paper, and as I read it again, I was shocked. All the dreams that had come bubbling up as I'd written —everything I thought ministry should be — had absolutely no connection to what I was doing."

No one can keep that up for long. Says Carolyn Weese,

for many years a staff member at Hollywood Presbyterian Church: "The joy of serving the church slowly gave way to 'my career at the church,' then to 'my job at the church,' to 'I'm in a rut and how do I get out of it?' "

Great Expectations

Why is it that many ministers can't do what they're gifted and called to do?

Usually because they are under tremendous expectations to do everything.

Maynard Nelson, pastor of Calvary Lutheran Church in Golden Valley, Minnesota, knows the feeling: "The ministry today is so demanding: We are to be administrators, counselors, managers of sometimes large budgets, preachers and teachers — the expectations are unreal."

Most pastors today, unlike those even fifty years ago, are expected to be jacks-of-all-trades, and too often, the sheer number of those trades forces them to be masters of none. Says a pastor from Southern California: "It's discouraging when you know you're not doing your best, when time won't allow you to study the way you want to study or to minister the way you want to minister. You go home in the evening and you've filled up your day, but you really haven't done anything."

It's not surprising that leads to discouragement. Says a Presbyterian minister: "Like most pastors, I sense a need to be omnicompetent. And then I fail in a particular area in which I'm not gifted. It's discouraging."

"If I could, I'd be with people hour after hour," laments another pastor. "That's the most important thing I could do. But you can't do it and administrate; you can't do it and be a good staff person."

An East Coast pastor explains the tension. "In seminary I was prepared for the life of a specialist," he says. "In the parish I had to become a generalist. I'm involved with administrative duties, committees, staff relationships, budgets, building programs, and on and on. I'd rather specialize in study and one-on-one care of people."

Some of the highest encouragers on the LEADERSHIP survey were preaching, preparing to preach, and leading worship. They're duties that refresh; they're close to the heart of ministers.

One of the greatest discouragers was doing church administration.

In many cases, the schedule seems to pit Administration vs. Sermon. Paradoxically, studying and preparing to preach puts a pastor in the office, behind a desk, working with paper, just as administration does. But the two have radically different effects. Since the two tasks are so closely tied to ministers' sense of encouragement, it's worth considering each of them more closely.

Why Is Administrating Enervating?

One reason that managing a congregation is so draining comes from the very nature of the church. The church is a volunteer organization, and there's no more difficult group to run, as Ted Engstrom, president emeritus of World Vision, points out: "A profit-making organization is the easiest to run. It's a business with a narrow measuring stick for success — profit. The next easiest to run is a nonprofit organization like World Vision. We pay our people. We can hire. We can release. There are more problems than with a profit company, but we still have a strong measure of control. Running a volunteer organization like the church is the hardest. The church accepts everyone, warts and all. Yet you're challenging these people to difficult ministry — without pay."

Civil War general William Tecumseh Sherman discovered what pastors have found when he had to command forces consisting of available home guards and volunteers. "I never did like to serve with volunteers," he reflected later, "because instead of being governed, they govern."

That's true no matter how good an administrator someone

is. Says one Reformed Church in America pastor: "Administration of the board of the church, even when successfully done, is often with personal pain."

A second enervating factor in administration is that it pulls you away from one-on-one ministry to people, where you're most likely to find encouragement. Yes, you may be working constantly with people, but not necessarily in close, refreshing ways. "When I'm down, it's probably because I haven't been with people; I haven't been hearing positive things about what's going on in the ministry," says an Evangelical Free Church minister. "But the larger the church grows, the more you're involved in administration, so you tend to move away from the personal contact with people. You don't get to hear the stories of what God has been doing."

Further, no matter how well a pastor administrates, he or she may not feel great personal reward from it. The (rare) compliment one gets for it doesn't mean as much as "That sermon really changed the way I've been looking at things."

Managing the Managing

What happened to Eugene Peterson that night seventeen years ago when he told his Session he wanted to quit? Is there hope for others who have reached the same emotional point?

Eugene picks up the story: "They thought for a moment and then said, 'Let *us* run the church.' After we talked it through the rest of the evening, I finally said okay.

"Two weeks later the stewardship committee met, and I walked into the meeting uninvited. The chairman of the group looked at me and asked, 'What's the matter? Don't you trust us?'

"I admitted, 'I guess I don't, but I'll try.' I turned around and walked out. It took a year to learn to trust God to call and use the men and women around me in ministry.

"I do moderate the Session. And I tell other committees that if they want me to come for a twenty-minute consultation on a specific problem I'll be happy to do that. But I haven't been to a committee meeting now, except in that capacity, for seventeen years."

There are some drawbacks to stepping back from administration, as Eugene will attest. Some things don't get done as well or as quickly. But the lesson in his experience is that pastors — even solo pastors, like him — can actually *hand off some administrative responsibilities* in order to grab firmer hold of pastoral ones. It's not easy, and not every pastor will approach it in the same way, but it can be done.

The pastor, however, still "has to make sure administration gets done," Eugene admits, even if he or she doesn't do it directly. That means for him, among other things, "I return telephone calls promptly. I answer my mail quickly. I put out a weekly newsletter. If you want to keep your job, people have to believe the church is running okay."

A second principle comes through a helpful distinction made by Ben Patterson, pastor of Irvine (California) Presbyterian Church. He asks, "What is the business of the church?" and answers by saying, "Actually there are two kinds of business." There is the Big-B Business — worship, the care of souls, helping people to mature in Christ. Then there is the little-b business — the budgets, committees, and programs that make all that possible. "The trick," he says, "is to keep the little-b business little." Paradoxically, that may come about by concentrating on it, by *learning to do the little-b business more quickly and efficiently.* For many pastors, such as Stan Allaby, minister at Black Rock Congregational Church in Fairfield, Connecticut, that has meant taking some American Management Association courses. For other pastors, it has meant reading Peter Drucker. Says Donald Seibert, retired chief executive officer of J. C. Penney, "I believe many pastors would surprise themselves by discovering what good administrators and managers they really are."

Gary Downing says he finds help in "managing the managing" by *focusing on a concept.* "You provide administration as much by being able to distill things for people into a single, burning idea — a bull's-eye for a target — as you do by creating programs. That's been a way for me to stay alive in ministry, because concepts last; they transcend programs. In my case, the concept has been the passage in 2 Corinthians 5 about being friendmakers for God. As I communicate that to people, it helps to give focus and direction — things that good administration does."

Many pastors have gained strength from seeing their administrative duties *as ministry itself*, rather than an interruption of it, as David Leucke and Samuel Southard argue for persuasively in their book *Pastoral Administration*. "We presume to show how administration can become a source of pastoral joy," the authors write. "Personal satisfaction can arise from making . . . administrative work serve fundamental ministry purposes."[2] Communicating, organizing, putting out fires — as tiring as this service is, it helps build the body of Christ. It's a portion of what it means "to prepare God's people for works of service" (Eph. 4:12).

Finally, ministers with whom I talked handle the discouraging aspects of their administrative duties by tying a counterweight to them — the joys of preaching and leading worship. They focus their concentration on these, and the emotional encouragement they receive continues to lift them through the week. We turn now to them.

The Strenuous Joy

According to the pastors who responded to the LEADERSHIP survey, preaching is one of the most buoying of duties.

Not that it isn't strenuous. Robert Hudnut, pastor of First Presbyterian Church in Winnetka, Illinois, describes the tension that builds: "I often wonder why I subject myself to Saturday nights. It's like a term paper and final exam every week."

And yet, he says, "On Sunday afternoon, even though I'm pretty tired, I get out the Bible and start on the next week. I find myself being reinvigorated, reenergized. I get new emotional energy as the Bible begins to course through me again.

Working in the Word brings me back up emotionally. It has its own inner momentum."

In general, even when you're discouraged, there's no better place to be than the pulpit. That's where the pastoral gifts God has given can be expressed most fully and used most effectively. It's where you can see and hear some reward for your efforts. In a wonderful, inexplicable way, that's where God's grace connects pastor and people, your gifts and their needs. What else can you do but rejoice in that?

Says John Yates, rector of The Falls Church (Episcopal) in suburban Washington: "When you come out of the pulpit and sense there's a hush over the congregation and God has used you in spite of yourself, in spite of your inadequacy, in spite of your own questions — that's exhilarating; that's humbling; that's really encouraging.

"Not long ago a man in our church taught a class on stewardship, and he stood up and said, 'You know, I'd never dealt with stewardship until one day when the pastor preached a sermon on tithing and hit me right between the eyes. I'd never heard that message before. I got angry. I got upset. But I went home and God dealt with me, and I knew it was right. My life has been different ever since.'

"When I heard him say that, I thought, *Wow! This must be God's blessing!*"

---

1. Gaylord Noyce, "Administration As Ministry: Taking the Long View," *The Christian Ministry* (March 1987), 13 – 15.
2. David S. Leucke and Samuel Southard, *Pastoral Administration: Integrating Ministry and Management in the Church* (Waco, Tex.: Word, 1986), 13.

SIX

I'M FACING A FEW DIFFICULT MEMBERS

A preacher's biggest problem is how to toughen his hide without hardening his heart.

VANCE HAVNER

As Gary Milam (not his real name) looked out over the Sunday morning congregation during the offertory hymn, his heart began to lift. Even some of the front pews were filled; it looked like the best attendance since he'd arrived six months ago. Welcoming the two new families earlier in the service had also been a boost. They were both excited about the church, and that rubbed off on him. He looked at his watch: *Twenty after eleven.* It was going to be a good message this morning; he could feel it.

His associate, Karl, leaned over toward him to say something, and Gary tilted his head that way while still looking out at the congregation.

"Gary," Karl said, "I'm going to take some time at the end of the service. I'm turning in my resignation."

Gary turned and looked at him. Two or three times Karl had made veiled comments about resigning, but still, coming in the middle of the service like this, it caught Gary completely off guard. "Are you sure that's what you want to do?" Gary whispered, searching his eyes.

"I'm sure," Karl said. He kept a steady gaze.

Gary knew he couldn't bodily stop him. "I'd ask that you not do that."

"It's time."

The offertory hymn was in its final chords. Gary stood, gave one more glance at Karl, and moved toward the pulpit. It was time to preach.

During the sermon Gary felt utterly schizophrenic. One part of him was looking at his notes and interacting with the congregation. But a deeper part inside his mind was trying to sort out what Karl's surprise move was going to mean.

Actually, he'd known things were brewing, especially after Thursday evening's deacons' meeting. Some opposition to Gary had begun to surface in the congregation, and one man had brought his grievances to the meeting. The deacons had fielded the charges well, Gary thought, but what had bothered him was Karl's silent nonsupport.

Since then he'd heard that Karl had never recovered from serving as interim pastor for six months and then being passed over for Gary. Karl's wife, especially, felt he should be senior pastor, the story went, and Karl had been increasingly a sounding board for the opposition. *This is probably the best thing that could happen, given all that,* Gary thought as he led into his closing prayer.

Gary said something to the congregation about "a short message from our minister of education before we close the service," nodded at Karl, and then walked over and sat down. Karl stepped to the pulpit, grabbed it on both sides, and began, "I regret that I must tell you I am resigning from First Church today." He stopped, waited for the sudden silence to punctuate the statement, and then kept going. Karl rambled some, but two phrases hit Gary between the eyes: "Carolyn and I have been mistreated by the church leadership," and "I have felt that, as a minister of the gospel, I can no longer serve when I have been asked to do things that violate my conscience."

Gary was stunned. He didn't know what Karl was alluding to, but he knew he'd never be able to repair the damage to his reputation if this kept up. He finally decided, at the six- or seven-minute mark, that as embarrassing as it would be, he was going to have to ask Karl to stop. He just wanted the service to end, but he couldn't witness the assassination of his character any longer. Just as he got ready to stand, Karl ended with, "Of course, the church will have to vote on whether to accept this or not. I leave my fate in your hands."

Sweet move, Gary thought. *Way to start an all-out war.*

Just then, Elmer Brownley, the church's grandfather deacon, stood. "Brother Pastor, I want to say a word," he said in that genteel Southern way of his. Gary motioned him to come forward. *If anybody can settle things down, it's Elmer,* Gary thought.

But Elmer, with his winsome, flowery style, finally ended with, "I move we not accept our dear brother Karl's resignation." About twenty people on the left side broke out clapping.

Now Gary was frightened. He looked out at the two new families, and he could see the puzzled, tense look in their eyes. Things were getting completely out of hand. He moved to the pulpit, took a deep breath, and tried to be the most soothing diplomat he'd ever been. "We appreciate your support of the church's leadership, Elmer," he began, "and we want to handle this in the right way. But since we're not in business session, such a motion is out of order. We'll have to address it in the appropriate forum." Elmer's face turned red and angry. *Well, I've cooked my goose with him,* Gary thought. But he was finally able to dismiss the service.

Karl did decide to resign. But that was not the end of the matter. First, a deacons' meeting that was called to discuss Karl's resignation became a forum on whether to support *Gary.* But the secret ballot went nine to one in Gary's favor.

That didn't end the trouble, though. Two or three people set up appointments with Gary to tell him, angrily, that he should resign. One Sunday, as he walked through the foyer to go into the sanctuary for the service, a man planted both feet in front of him and called him a liar loud enough for everyone to hear. A petition asking for his resignation began to circulate. That didn't get anywhere, so another petition saying "We want to promote peace and unity and harmony in the church, so we want to poll the church about their satisfaction with the current leadership" made the rounds. That ultimately led to a strong vote in favor of Gary by the congregation.

After the congregational meeting, two families left immediately, and then about ten more over the next couple months.

"At that point, I was ready to quit," he says. "I was beaten to a pulp. I had responded to my critics until it had sapped all my spiritual energy. I was having a tough time trying to preach."

While Gary was thinking about leaving, though, he went to a Bible study seminar on Philippians. "I saw what a pastor's heart really was," he says. "I determined I was going to develop a new relationship with my people regardless of how they responded. Then I made a fresh commitment to studying and preaching the Word; I'd get my mind off my problem and focus on the Scriptures. I came back and began a series in Philippians, and I saw that Paul was rejoicing in circumstances he didn't deserve and didn't desire. That helped change my attitude, and I think that did more to change the church than anything. There's something about attacking someone who's peaceful that just takes all the fun out of it."

Now, he says, things have turned around.

The criticism has stopped. Recently ten people have become Christians and joined the church. Attendance continues to grow, and the congregation has united behind a major building program.

Small Numbers, Huge Impact

As the story above illustrates, a few troublesome members, even when they are placated or eventually leave, halt ministry. They wound people, they divide churches, and they deeply discourage pastors.

"A few vocal members" are probably the leading cause of pastoral resignations. Even when the handful of troublesome members doesn't force a pastor out, it makes his or her life miserable. Though the group is invariably small, its impact is disproportionately large.

For one thing, *critical comments carry more weight than positive ones.* Ninety-nine people can tell us how meaningful our sermon was to them, but if only one person says, "It just didn't hit me today," that's the comment we'll likely be dwelling on at two o'clock that afternoon.

Pastors, whose focus is caring for people, *may be particularly vulnerable to verbal attacks.* "I'm a very sensitive individual," admits a Lutheran pastor, "and I tend to take things personally. So every time someone says something critical about me, I really struggle through the process to see whether it's applicable." And when a few people kick up dust, or decide to leave, no matter how wrong or spiteful they were, some pastors feel a sense of failure.

One writes: "The vice-chairman of the church board had 'strong disagreements with the direction the church is taking.' I didn't make the adjustments he felt were needed, so he convened three other families weekly to 'pray for the spiritual life of the church.' These families then petitioned our board of deacons to examine me about specific doctrinal issues, like my views of demons, and the geographic location of heaven. The deacons approved my views, so the vice-chairman then petitioned our district executive committee to conduct a similar review. The committee approved my views, but he still didn't give up. He petitioned for a hearing by the entire district board. They supported me as well, so he finally left the church and took the three families with him. But I was emotionally drained. I 'won,' but I also felt I had failed as a pastor to meet the needs of these families."

There's a final reason why a handful of disgruntled members seems like an army. Often the few are powerful personalities, and so *the rest of the church,* which may actually support the pastor, *doesn't want to stand up to them.* Wrote one pastor on the survey: "I presently have a family who fights my ministry. No matter what I do, it is wrong, and most of their criticism is shared with other members of the congregation behind my back. What really hurts, however, is not their criticism and personal attacks, but the lack of support I feel from the local power structure." When the congregational majority becomes the "silent majority," pastors feel all alone. "My leadership style led to conflict with a very dominant figure in the congregation who wanted everything done his way," tells one minister. "I felt for a time that all the other church folk left me to fight the battle alone. The lack of support from those I thought were behind me brought me my greatest sense of discouragement ever in ministry."

The pernicious aspect of dealing with the few troublesome members is that they pull a pastor away from the essential work of ministry. Robert Norris, pastor of Fourth Presbyterian Church in Bethesda, Maryland, knows the difficulty: "You spend more time with those people, and it becomes a drain on you. It's a constant discouragement, because you know what you should be doing is building up those who are going forward, encouraging them. But instead, you're spending more and more time with the sick and less and less with the well and willing. You betray your call to equip."

Survival Strategies

Pastors across the country *have* found ways to deal with the few difficult members, however. Though some church leaders have learned through great pain or resignation, they have discovered strategies for not only surviving the few vocal parishioners but actually ministering to them. Here are veteran pastors' insights.

Accept the fact that such people not only can, but will, be part of every church. "I once believed it *possible* that a church might bring suffering to a minister," writes Lynn Anderson, for the past sixteen years minister of the Highland Church of Christ in Abilene, Texas. "I now believe it is *inevitable*." It's not easy, though, to accept the fact that Christians can act in such hurtful ways. A LEADERSHIP survey in 1981 found that a stunning 85 percent of pastors had at one point in their professional lives "felt betrayed by persons I thought I could trust," yet only a few said they'd anticipated that anything like this could happen. Says Maynard Nelson: "When I started in the ministry, I naively believed that all the church members would be supporting me and praying for me and that we would be seeking to reach out to the world. The forces of evil were 'out there.' It was a disillusionment, then, when I found that sometimes the church members were the greatest problem to deal with. It wasn't the world out there, it was rather petty things, bickering, and factions within the church. But it helped as I gradually came to realize that really, the church is human, but in it God has chosen to reveal his love and grace and mercy."

Try to focus on the supportive majority. It's hard but essential to remember that the few vocal members really are few. Though two families are disgruntled, another thirty may be quite pleased with your ministry. One Presbyterian pastor from the South said he was helped by the counsel of a friend who is an insurance agent. "He told me he had learned in his training the 'Rule of the 5 Percent,' which says that no matter what you do, approximately 5 percent of your insurance clients aren't going to be happy. So don't sweat them. Well, it's just about the same in the church." This kind of thinking helped one pastor, who wrote: "The *key* family, the ones who started the church, expressed major dissatisfaction with my ministry and announced they were leaving the church. I had invested a large amount of time with this family, they had been my strongest supporters and affirmers, and now they turned on me and left. But I decided to stay because I realized they were only one family. The rest of the church was so positive I figured it was better to stay."

A third strategy is to *weigh your critics*, which means discerning between a member offering valid criticism and the one who's a destructive force in the church. What's the line between an aggressive person and the "divisive person" Paul warned so strongly against? Most pastors, rightly so, tend to give difficult members the benefit of the doubt, to tolerate them and be patient with them. But when is it time for a pastor to take a strong hand, for both the peace of the church and the ultimate spiritual growth of the uncharitable person?

Truman Dollar, pastor of Temple Baptist Church in the Detroit suburb of Redford, makes this distinction: "Disunity . . . comes from people who are acting autonomously, who are not obeying the Scripture: 'Let this mind be in you which was also in Christ Jesus.'. . . There's a big difference between being autonomous and being a strong, independent thinker, what I call being 'secure in Christ.' People who are secure in Christ offer some of the brightest and most helpful ideas for the growth of the church. And they can be aggressive.

"But here's the difference: They offer ideas, do homework, take initiative, and still maintain the mind of Christ. When the body has made its decision, they don't continue to lobby or create dissent. The autonomous person, on the other hand, maintains his position long after the vote and says, 'You're all wrong.' "

An Alabama pastor expands on the ways he knows when a critic is becoming more destructive than constructive: "I can tell when I have accepted their criticism and acted on it, when I have truly changed or improved what they were criticizing. Then I watch: Do they shift to carping about something else so they're *never* satisfied? And are they willing to themselves accept correction? If not, then, as harsh as it sounds, I recognize they have a 'poisonous bite,' and I need to deal with them in a different, firmer, way than I do others."

But for members who do not fall into this tiny group, most pastors suggest really *listening to them*.

One pastor who learned to listen to his critics was John Yates. "This church is a very historic church; George Washington was on the vestry that built the building," he says. "So when I came to this church and began to suggest changes, not everyone was pleased. About a year after I'd been here I had an annual review, and all kinds of criticism came out. That was hard, but I came back from that and suggested a 'rector's advisory committee' of five people from our vestry. I said, 'Can we meet together at least once a month? Any way in which I am coming across to the congregation as arrogant or unthoughtful or insensitive, will you please tell me? Tell me what people are saying, because lots of times I think there may be miscommunication. And if I am leading in a way that's counterproductive, I want you to tell me.'

"They thought it was a wonderful idea. So for about five years we met one Saturday morning each month. Sometimes a person would say, 'John, I heard that you did so-and-so, and I'd like to tell you, if you handled it that way, you blew it.' There were people on the committee whom I had a real hard time with. And they had a real hard time with me. But meeting was such a help. I would ask their advice about how to handle a pastoral problem or leadership problem, and we got to be close, with frank communication. As a result, nine times out of ten I was able to nip a problem in the bud."

Develop "sensitive calluses." A United Church of Christ minister expresses his frustration: "It pays off sometimes for me to be insensitive, to let the water run off my back like a duck's. But I've been surprised that even the most educated, successful, and sophisticated people in my congregation are terribly fragile. If I'm not sensitive, I can't minister to them."

One helpful insight to this problem came from a pastor who went through a church split because of a few vocal members. "I was an associate for a while with a pastor who used to brag about his 'shoe-leather skin.' I didn't want to have to have that, but as I looked around I couldn't see how you could survive without it. Every older pastor I knew was tough and rough and callous and a little bit bitter.

"But then I met this one pastor who had been through all kinds of hell in his congregation, and yet he was gracious and humble and gentle; he'd ended up sweet. I thought to myself, *So there is a way.* But I didn't know what it was. I was talking with a friend who is a pianist one day about this, and he said to me, 'Eric, maybe this will help. As a pianist, there are two things I want. I want sensitivity in my fingers so I can feel the keys, but I also need them calloused enough so that I can play for a long time.' Ever since, I've been trying to develop sensitive calluses."

Remember that God can use "what is meant for evil as good." "I came from a church where for nine years I really didn't know any criticism," says one West Coast pastor, "to here, where in two years I've had more criticism than in my whole life. One thing that's helped me is that old phrase, 'You either get bitter or you get better.' I have a choice. I keep trying to say, 'I'm not going to let this thing make me bitter. By God's grace this situation is going to make me better.' "

One pastor said the only way he could endure criticism was to "consider him who endured such opposition from sinful men, so that you will not grow weary and lose heart" (Heb. 12:3). The key is focusing on Jesus, on remembering his love and faithfulness and commitment.

"Sometimes I'd call my former senior pastor," says one minister, "and pour out to him all the criticism I was getting, all the miscommunication that was happening, all the ways people were misinterpreting my motives. He'd listen, and then he'd say, 'Oh, do I understand. John, God's making a man out of you. God's about a great work, you know.' That would sort of bring me back and refresh me and encourage me. I hadn't been able to see it, but God was at work."

From Break You to Make You

"A congregation can either make you or break you" is a saying that a few difficult members demonstrate clearly. But what about the members who *make* a pastor, the ones who encourage, who make it all seem worthwhile?

Often pastors mentioned just one or two people as giving them all the encouragement they needed to keep going. Just as it takes only a few difficult members to drive a pastor crazy, it takes only a few delightful ones to keep him or her sane. The bright, positive, forward-looking members also have a disproportionate impact on the church. The people who come to Christ, who really change, who give up destructive habits, who learn to reach out — these may be only a handful, but they bring armloads of encouragement.

The LEADERSHIP survey asked pastors to identify a time when they felt, "If for no other reason, this is why I want to stay in the ministry." Many of the answers told of a specific person and how he or she had grown in grace through the pastor's ministry. Reading the answers is encouraging in itself:

• "I had preached a series of sermons on prayer, and later I found out that it had helped the prayer life of one of our oldest members. It was a thrill seeing God use his Word to change the lives of people."

• "Over a period of fifteen years I saw several members of the same family come to Christ and begin to grow spiritually."

• "A student came to know the Lord, and now she tells others about it, as a direct result of my life touching hers."

• "A young man I had helped through and after an emotional breakdown decided to go on to a Christian college."

• "In one marriage, the husband had moved out, and the wife was despondent, terrified, and bitter. The husband and wife agreed the children were better off with one parent than two at war. Over time I was able to establish ground rules for communication, stress management, and so on. The husband and wife are now back together, and the children have two loving parents. And the parents love their pastor."

A key characteristic of a congregation's encouraging people is that they are grateful. One pastor wrote of his most encouraging moment in the ministry: "A young mother, reared in our church, moved with her family to another town and church. Upon returning, she told me, 'I have come to the conclusion that you are one of the best, true-to-the-Bible teachers I've ever heard. Thank you for teaching me and my family God's Word.' "

Wrote another: "I asked a woman why she had gotten

saved, expecting some theological response. Instead, she said, 'Because I wanted to be like you and your wife.' "

You can go a long way on a comment like that.

In fact, it was because of such a comment that one pastor is even in the ministry today. "One night while in seminary," he wrote, "I told my wife I was thinking of throwing in the towel. The phone rang then, and I found out a deacon from our home church was in the hospital for tests, and it was almost surely cancer. I called him to cheer him up, and while we were talking, he said, 'We sure do miss you here. But we know that God has bigger and better things for you.' "

Maximizing Ministry to the Encouragers

So within each congregation there are various types of people, and some tend to lift a pastor and move a ministry forward. Others tend to pin a pastor down and hinder the church's mission.

No pastor, of course, can completely exempt himself or herself from ministry to the more discouraging members. And indeed, none would probably want to. Though more draining to shepherd, these sheep are no less a part of the flock, and pastors feel a call — perhaps an extra urgency — to help and care for them. "It just so happens that the church is the place where very difficult people hang out," says one minister, "but rightfully so. That's where they should be."

But recognizing that, what practical things can be done to maximize ministry to the well and willing? Here are ways pastors have found to spend more of their energy where it's more productive and, thus, be more encouraged:

Monitor where your time is being spent. One pastor suggests taking a datebook from the last month and candidly evaluating which kind of people you've been spending the most time with. Whether you choose that method or not, pastors have found their ministry more effective and encouraging as they've been somewhat conscious of where they're investing their time. "I see it as following Paul's command in Ephesians

5 to 'not live as unwise but wise, making the most of every opportunity,' " says Jim Bankhead, pastor of First Presbyterian Church in Opelika, Alabama.

Spend time with people on a project you love. Ministers said their spirits have been buoyed when they carved time from their schedule for a ministry area they were specially interested in — say, helping the poor, reaching college students, building strong marriages. The people who join the pastor on the project tend to share the pastor's vision and enthusiasm. As a result, the ministry moves forward, which is encouraging in itself. But as important for the pastor is that for at least one hour each week you're with people who resonate with your interests.

John Yates, for example, has long had an interest — partly because he has five children of his own — in helping Christian families. So about five years ago he asked several married couples if they would like to meet with him and his wife, Susan, for a semester to study Christian family life. He wasn't quite sure what would happen, but they began meeting every other week for several months. The result? "They drew things out of me and my wife we hadn't anticipated. We were able to minister to them, teach them, in a special way. In fact, we were so encouraged by what happened that we decided we would try to extend the experience to others." The church has since started many of these Family Life Action Groups, and other churches have reproduced the idea. A powerful ministry came about because John invested at least some time each week in a favorite area. And as a fringe benefit, "the groups have turned out to be a great encouragement" to him.

Give people opportunities to tell how God has been working in their lives. Chuck Smalley, associate pastor at Wayzata (Minnesota) Evangelical Free Church, explains the dynamic: "The thing that attracted me to ministry was being involved with people, and the thing that keeps me in ministry is seeing people's lives change. So it was exciting last month at a banquet for the people in our small groups. We had five or six people stand and share the benefits of being in a small group. One or two were from a small group for older singles, and they'd been divorced and really gone through a lot of pain. To hear them tell how God has changed their lives, and how their small group is one of the most important things in their lives, made me want to keep going."

In a sense, each of these steps is a way for the pastor to allow people to minister to him or her. Through them "the whole body . . . grows and builds itself up in love, as each part does its work" (Eph. 4:16).

Placing Our Feet

I asked one church leader, "How can we minister to the few difficult members without letting them utterly discourage us or cut off ministry to the others?"

"In ministry," he responded, "my one foot may become pinned to the earth, caught in the difficulties of the moment. But don't forget: I have another foot. And I try to keep that one planted in heaven."

SEVEN

I NEED AFFIRMATION FOR WHAT I DO

I can live for two months on a good compliment.

MARK TWAIN

Find rest, O my soul, in God alone; my hope comes from him.

You, O Lord, are loving. Surely you will reward each person according to what he has done.

DAVID (Psalm 62:5, 12)

Several years ago Dr. Frederick Herzberg, professor of management at the University of Utah, set out to discover what factors encouraged employees and what factors discouraged them. As he studied workers in a variety of settings, he found that despite the diverse situations, specific factors emerged clearly as the top encouragers. In the *Harvard Business Review*, he listed them.

The top encourager Dr. Herzberg discovered: Achievement.

The second greatest encourager: Recognition.[1]

Doing something well — and then being recognized for it — there is no greater motivator. The sweetness of heaven will be, in part, hearing the words of the one for whom we have worked say, "Well done, good and faithful servant!" Yet these top two human energizers — achievement and recognition — come rarely for some pastors. "There are long stretches when I don't hear anything such as 'We really do understand what you're doing; we appreciate it,' " says a large-church pastor. "In the middle of those long dry spells, it can be discouraging. Like a radio deejay, I wonder, *Is anybody out there? Is anybody really listening?*"

No News Is Bad News

When feedback does come, whether positive or negative, it's often in the form of vague and general impressions — the least helpful kind. How are you supposed to change when you hear "We're just not being fed" (whatever that means) or even "That sermon touched me, Pastor"? No specific weaknesses have been identified to work on, no specific strengths to build on. The comments leave you with a free-floating sense of frustration.

Part of the problem is that few people understand the work of the pastor well enough to evaluate it helpfully. Says a Baptist pastor in the Midwest: "The laity don't really know what we do. They can give some feedback on our personal relationships with them, but they're not following us around, seeing how we led the music committee meeting or how we handled hospital visitation yesterday. So it can get lonely wondering how you're doing.

"Of course, when I'm honest, I'm not sure I want to hear a lot of feedback. Well, I would like to hear positive feedback, but I'm not sure I want to hear a lot of negative."

The result is that for the solo pastor, especially, there may be long stretches "where seldom is heard an encouraging word." Without affirmation, some pastors withdraw. Admits one, "It's not a good way to handle it, but if I articulate something we need to do and everyone looks at me cockeyed, I just back off. I withdraw and say, *The heck with it.*" Another natural response is to become even more dependent on the stray comment that comes our way.

Is there a way to get support and affirmation without becoming dependent on "the praise of men"? How can you get clear and helpful feedback on how you're doing — and weather the times when you don't get any? Says Steve Harris: "Ed Koch, the mayor of New York, is famous for walking around saying, 'How'm I doin'?' That's his pet phrase: 'How'm I doin'?' I've thought it would be good if we as pas-

tors could do that once in a while."
But is it possible?
Here's what tenured pastors had to say.

Finding Feedback without Fishing

By teaching the congregation how to encourage each other, the pastor also gains encouragement, H. B. London has learned. The First Church of the Nazarene in Pasadena, California, places "encouragement cards" in the pews and asks members to use them to write uplifting notes to others in the congregation and then place them in the offering plate. The church office then fills out the addresses for the intended recipients and mails the cards. And as a fringe benefit, London and the staff often receive cards themselves. When I visited the church not long ago, several bulletin boards in the church office had encouragement cards pinned to them. H. B. shared this one he'd received: "I wanted to take the opportunity to tell you I'm very glad you are our pastor. When you preach I sort of feel like you and I are having our own little conversation, and that feels good. Thanks." When a congregation learns to be encouraging, pastors benefit the most.

Giving people a chance to tell how God has been working in their lives also opens the gates for affirmation (and builds an affirming climate in the congregation). One pastor wrote on the LEADERSHIP survey: "After preaching on transformation I invited volunteers to stand and tell how they had experienced transformation during that year. As they stood and told how the Lord had changed their lives, it was the greatest day of encouragement I ever had in the ministry." Why restrict such testimonials to an anniversary? They glorify God, build up the church — and remind you that God really is working through your ministry.

To get more concrete evaluation, some pastors have employed periodic questionnaires or surveys. Not long ago, John Vawter, pastor of Wayzata (Minnesota) Evangelical Free

Church, mailed evaluation forms to thirty-five people in his congregation to measure his preaching effectiveness. John got back a few responses that stung, but those helped him improve specific areas such as projecting his voice more during the introduction and building rapport by not using anecdotes that pointed to the congregation's frailties.

Another pastor distributes annual "performance profiles" to a dozen key lay leaders for their evaluation of his previous year's effectiveness. Others use similar measures, though less formal, with a pastoral relations committee.

Despite measures like these, long stretches of silence may come. Some pastors have compensated with the knowledge that not all churches are affirming by nature. Says a pastor in the upper Midwest: "This church is not an affirming church, as a culture. Maybe it's the Midwest reserve, the Scandinavian heritage, or simply that people were never really trained how to express what they're feeling. Then we have the suburban mentality that says, 'Everything's always fine.' But if a pastor here based his staying on people's affirmation of his pulpit ministry, he'd never last.

"Somehow recognizing that helps, though. It doesn't solve the problem of where you get encouragement, but it at least helps you to understand it's not going to come, in this case, from a lot of individuals in the church."

This holds true particularly for pastors who have just moved from a loving parish to one that is more reserved or even standoffish. As a temporary measure, at least, contact with people in a previous work can remind you that you have been appreciated and probably will be again. A pastor in the mid-Atlantic states discovered this: "I've had the opportunity to go back to churches where I had served as a pastor. The thing that impressed me the most was the number of people who were able to mention times in their lives when I was present with them in the midst of their particular needs."

Many pastors accomplish the same thing by saving their notes of encouragement and going back to them on gray days.

"You pull some of them out, and you get a different perspective," smiles John Yates. "Here's one I've kept. 'Dear John: We think you're great; we think you're great; we think you're great! Roger loves you, I love you, God loves you. You can do all things through Christ. Love, Roger and Julie.' "

A note like that becomes an Ebenezer, an unbudgeable monument that declares you are indeed doing a work that counts.

In the final analysis, though, as Alabama pastor Jim Bankhead puts it, "If your staying power depends on other people's affirmation, you'd never stay in some places. The pastors I know who have been able to stay with little or no recognition have done so because they had a vital relationship with Christ. His approval sustains you when there is no other."

Salary Setbacks

Affirmation comes in both verbal and nonverbal forms. The verbal, as stimulating as it is, needs the nonverbal, most often shown through finances, to support it. And when a verbal message disagrees with a nonverbal one, people will believe the nonverbal one every time. No matter how much a pastor hears he or she is loved, unless reflected in some way financially, the words begin to sound hollow.

Not long ago I learned of a pastor who had led his congregation from under one hundred members to five hundred in twenty years of just plain hard work. He had guided the church in a relocation and building project, which had been an enormous success. Yet in the twenty years he'd given to this church, he had received raises in only six of them. The pastor and his wife were now on the other side of midlife with no savings for retirement, and they'd had to borrow against the equity in their home to finance an education for their children, so they had little if any money left. What hurt him most, he admitted in a low moment, was seeing board members head off for expensive vacations while they told him he needed to tighten his belt. He was beginning to feel the people in the church didn't really appreciate a thing he'd done.

A staff member of a Conservative Baptist church of over a thousand members knew the feeling when he wrote, "The number one problem I face in my ministry is my lack of money compared to my load of responsibility." Another pastor confessed, "Those fleeting moments of thinking about leaving the ministry have come mostly as a result of low compensation." When you're not being affirmed financially, your checkbook may be hit hard, but your emotions will be hit even harder. According to a recent Gallup poll commissioned by the Christian Broadcasting Network, the most common reasons for depression were job-related pressures and financial problems, or in other words, heavy work and light pay. The study by Dr. Frederick Herzberg mentioned earlier concurs: a leading cause of discouragement for employees is an inadequate salary.

Almost four of every ten respondents to the LEADERSHIP survey said their compensation discouraged them. The reason the problem is so widespread can be easily documented.

Based on data culled from the 1985 Bureau of Labor Statistics, Leonard Sweet writes: "Among professionals only nursery school and kindergarten teachers rank below clergy in median weekly earnings. Secretaries, truck drivers, office machine repairers, postal clerks, drywall installers and laboratory technicians all have weekly incomes higher than those of clergy. And none of them put in three to four years of graduate school after four years of college."[2]

Lyle Schaller points out that in the last fifty years, pastors' salaries have slid from the equivalent of a school district superintendent's, to a high school principal's, to a classroom teacher's. And self-esteem slides with them.

No one finds that an easy thing to come to grips with. As a pastor in his mid-thirties admitted: "I've already reached the peak of my earning power. It's going to be a flat curve for a long time now. It's tough to accept that, to be honest about what that means for my family, for me, for my self-esteem."

Affirmation without Affluence

Business executive Fred Smith says that a problem is something you can do something about; if you can't do something about it, it's a fact of life. In that case, feeling unaffirmed because of low compensation is both a problem and a fact of life. It's a problem in the sense that pastors have done, and can do, some things about it. But it's a fact of life because certain elements of it cannot be changed.

For example, it's an unchanging fact of life that asking for more money is risky and may well be misunderstood, as one pastor who completed the LEADERSHIP survey discovered through a painful experience. "We had just had a new baby and had another child in a long hospitalization," he writes. "But when I asked for a pay raise, it led to my firing. What really hurt was that one of those who voted against me was someone I had led to Christ and counted as a personal friend."

And yet, pastors have begun to overcome this source of discouragement as they've done the things they could do.

The internal outlook is where many pastors have concentrated their energies. They make it year to year by focusing not on their low pay but on God's call and the rewards he gives. "The church is not the highest-paying organization in the world," says one pastor, "and there's always that draw to material things, but my wife and I recognize it as a short-term sort of draw. It's not going to motivate you over the long haul."

Wrote a United Methodist pastor from the South: "Once I was invited by a businessman to go to work for him at three times the salary I was receiving." That offer would have lured many people from many careers, but this pastor added, "My definite call of God gave me the reason I must stay." Not that he's unhappy about that call. He said, "My choice is being a pastor of a local church. That is where the real action is."

His commitment reminded me of a story told by Tim Hansel: "A war correspondent tells a story of coming across a nun on her knees patiently swabbing the gangrenous leg of a very sick young soldier lying on a mat. Revulsed by the scene, he had to turn his head away. Finally he said to her, 'Sister, I wouldn't do that for a million dollars.'

"The nun paused momentarily, and said, 'Neither would I.' "[3]

But there may come a point where you have adjusted your outlook and considered your call and still come up feeling unappreciated and unaffirmed — or just plain unable to make ends meet. Then it's time, pastors have discovered — if only for the sake of your relationship with the people — to take a deep breath and ask for more. Nobody finds that easy; it's full of self-examination and just plain fear. But it can prevent the smoldering bitterness that comes from trying to pour yourself out for people who seem either uncaring or unconcerned.

"It's hard to take that first step," explains Ed Bratcher. "We clergy feel very uncomfortable talking about money, partly because we still have some of the Middle Age concept that poverty is a virtue.

"In my first pastorate, a brand-new church in Austin, Texas, we were meeting in a barracks building. In my fifth year there I was feeling the need to get away for some continuing education. With the church being new, I wasn't sure how it would go, but finally with some fear and trepidation I went to the deacons and asked if they would provide for me to be gone three weeks that summer for a program I'd investigated.

"Not only were they unanimous in their support, they made the motion that continuing education be written into the budget every year. I had gone four years without asking for anything. But when I finally got up the courage to ask, people were very gracious.

"That incident came to mind recently," Ed continues, "when I was talking with a seminarian who was a staff person here. He was really feeling financially pressured, and I told him, 'You have got to tell the personnel committee exactly where you find yourself. Not that they will necessarily give you everything you need, but if you don't tell them, they are not going to know what your needs are.' He was reluctant. Finally I told him I wanted a written statement of his financial needs. He wrote it, and I pushed him to present it to the personnel committee.

"When he did, they were glad to give him what he needed."

Not every story of a pastor going to the board ends so happily, but many do. One pastor wrote on the LEADERSHIP survey that his greatest sense of encouragement in ministry is occurring right now, largely because he recently asked his board for an increase — and they responded with a 20 percent raise. Affirmation!

Some pastors who ask for what they need will be rebuffed. But their number is far smaller than the number of pastors who desperately need more, who feel unappreciated and unaffirmed, but fear to make their needs known. Larry Osborne, pastor of the North Coast Evangelical Free Church in Oceanside, California, is one pastor who has overcome that fear and been honest with his board about his financial needs. After several experiences, he reports, "When good people get the facts straight, the outcome is usually fair for all concerned."

The Toughest Critic of All

There's a third reason pastors cry, "I need affirmation for what I do," and it's a surprising one. The source of discouragement is not a silent congregation or an uncaring board. In fact, it's not a group at all. It's a single person.

This person often demands more than anyone else and can be severely critical. He or she can make it hard for a pastor to receive a genuine compliment.

The person's name is *I*.

A Lutheran pastor confessed to me, "I think the thing that

discourages me most — even more than the disloyalty of some of the people — is myself. My own sins and my own failures and my own faults — those are the ones that bother me." Said another minister: "People do place high expectations on clergy. But sometimes I'm the hardest on myself. I have great expectations, and then I don't live up to them. So I get down on myself."

Don Gerig, president of Fort Wayne Bible College, discovered this in his early years of ministry. "In my first fifteen years of ministry," he writes, "I let myself become a slave to the annual records I had to send the denomination. I couldn't let my number of baptisms or sermons slip. The more patients in the hospital, the better; I'd get more calls logged and help my statistics. I was running myself ragged for the sake of the record, not for ministry.

"The sad thing was I thought that's how ministry was supposed to be. My expectations, not the ministry needs, were creating the overwork."

Assessing Your Own Expectations

Self-expectations, like internal injuries, can be difficult to pinpoint. Something hurts, all right, but what? And how do you treat it?

Some pastors have found helpful the counsel of Louis McBurney, a Mayo Clinic–trained psychiatrist and founder of Marble Retreat, a counseling center for pastors and other Christian workers. McBurney advocates a four-step process to assess internal expectations and then set realistic goals.

The first step is to get in touch with expectations by completing sentences like:

"In my relationship with my wife, I expect to . . ."

"As a father, I expect myself to . . ."

"As a pastor, I won't be satisfied with my performance unless I . . ."

"The most important goals I have for myself as a person are . . ."

"It may be helpful to articulate these expectations to another person," McBurney writes. "You may be able to realistically assess your expectations alone, but it's very difficult."

The second step is to try to separate external expectations from internal ones. Says McBurney: "It often helps to ask, 'Where did that idea come from? When or where did I adopt that as a goal or expectation for myself? Does my congregation really expect this of me, or is most of it coming from within me?' "

Many pastors find their unrealistic self-expectations come from seeing highly gifted individuals at work. "We'd all like to think we're Dobson in the counseling room and Criswell in the pulpit," says one, "but we're not.

"I look at Criswell and marvel. People at First Baptist in Dallas don't say, 'We came in June of 1978'; they say, 'We came when Pastor Criswell was in Philippians.' I'd love to be able to preach like that. He can get on a theme and stay with it, and people are right with him. But if I try that, I kill it. If I preach any series longer than three months, people get tired of it.

"The only way I can keep from getting discouraged about that," he says, "is to come to grips with what my gifts are. I need to live within what God has given."

McBurney's third suggestion: "Compare your conscious goals and expectations against the unconscious motivators of anger, fear, and guilt." This kind of winnowing process helped a United Methodist pastor I talked to realize, "One reason I can't get everything done is my own fear of rejection. I'm afraid if I say no, people will reject me, and that makes me take on too much."

Finally, McBurney suggests, "Examine how closely your sense of self-worth is wrapped up in fulfilling your expectations."

Many pastors talk of discovering, often through painful experiences, that ultimately, self-worth comes from God alone. In the words of Christian psychologist David Bock,

"The acceptance of the self as lovable and worthwhile has its foundation in the mysterious reality that *God* is both the author and the revealer of man's worth."

Consider the experience of Richard Foster in his first church: "I had finished my doctorate, and I was supposed to be an expert. I went to a tiny church in Southern California that would rank as a marginal failure on the ecclesiastical scoreboards. I went in there and worked and planned and organized, determined to turn this church around. But things got worse. Anger seemed to permeate everyone: the conservatives were mad at the liberals, the liberals were mad at the radicals, and the radicals were mad at everyone else. I hated to go to pastors' conferences because I didn't have any success stories to tell. I was working myself to death, but it seemed to do no good. Then I spent three days with my spiritual director. Toward the end of that time he said, 'Dick, you have to decide whether you are going to be a minister of this church or a minister of Christ.' That was a turning point. Until then I had allowed other people's expectations — and my own — to manipulate me."

When our work and worth come from God, his grace covers when we fail. "My biggest failure as a minister is letting details slip by and not being faithful in doing the little things that need to be done," says a Lutheran pastor. "Once a funeral director called me and said, 'I have this person who's not a member of your church, but could you take the funeral?' I said okay.

"Some days later I went out to make some calls, and on the way I drove by the funeral parlor and saw all these cars there. All of a sudden I realized I had forgotten the funeral! I quickly called and the funeral director said, 'I got somebody else.'

"That was bad. Oh, it's hard to admit I did that. The only way I can deal with it is to go to Jesus."

Finding our worth in God and receiving our ultimate affirmation from him, paradoxically, frees us to truly receive affirmation from others. Writes Ed Bratcher: "I had the misconception that it was wrong to accept positive strokes for the good that I did — that I would become too proud and arrogant. . . . I have a hunch that ministers would experience greater fulfillment in ministry if they were able to accept more head patting from their congregation. A pastor who had left the ministry for a while told me that one reason he had decided to return to the parish ministry was that in his years as an ex-pastor he had learned how to receive positive strokes."[4] That's a wonderful lesson.

Michael Donald, pastor of Liberty Baptist Church in Van Wert, Ohio, finished preaching on a Sunday evening not long ago and dismissed the service. But then one of the men in the congregation came forward and said, "Wait, Pastor, we're not done yet. We need to do something." Then he and another man brought two high-back chairs to the front of the small, storefront church and had Michael and his wife sit in them. They looked at each other nervously, not quite sure what was going on.

"You know, we've had some hard times with pastors here," began one, "and some of those pastors discouraged a lot of people. But you have accepted us the way we are. And we wanted to let you know on your one-year anniversary that we love you."

Then one by one, spontaneously, members stood to tell the Donalds why they loved them and were glad the Lord had sent them their way.

"You haven't put a lot of expectations on us," said one person. "I'm so glad you've been willing to just be real before us," said another. Other people contributed other statements.

Mike went home that night ready to serve those several dozen people in a way he never had before. "It was my most encouraging moment in ministry," he says. "Ever."

1. Cited by John Cheydleur, "Burn-Out and Walk-Out," *Leadership* (Summer 1980), 62.
2. Leonard I. Sweet, "Pearlygate Satires Are Weak on Substance," *The Christian Century* (July 29 – August 5, 1987), 644 – 5.
3. Tim Hansel, *When I Relax I Feel Guilty* (Elgin, Ill.: David C. Cook, 1979), 127.
4. Edward B. Bratcher, *The Walk-On-Water Syndrome* (Waco, Tex.: Word, 1984), 115.

EIGHT

I NEED REST AND REFRESHMENT

God's Word refers to the Christian life often as a walk, seldom as a run, and never as a mad dash.

STEVEN J. COLE

In *When I Relax I Feel Guilty*, Tim Hansel writes of his years as a coach and area director for Young Life: "I would work twelve, fourteen, even fifteen hours a day, six or seven days a week. And I would come home feeling that I hadn't worked enough. So I tried to cram even more into my schedule. I spent more time promoting living than I did living."[1]

Many pastors know what Hansel's talking about: Long days, short breaks, and the increasing ugliness of being busy, what one called "doing more but enjoying it less."

One jumbled, crowded page on a Day-Timer follows another. One committee meeting leads to another. One sermon is hardly done when the next one looms ahead. A pastor captured the feeling when he described his weekly schedule as "an overstuffed glove compartment."

The husband of one minister felt this frustration when he wrote: "The overwhelming, indeed the single, issue is how to support my friend and love in a profession that makes extraordinary and high demands on every aspect of her life. My job is much less demanding, and I can walk away from it every afternoon. But a minister is a target for all the brokenness brought into the church by its people — lay and ordained. A minister is a workhorse trying to pull an overloaded wagon uphill."[2]

That load easily leads to burnout. Lutheran psychiatrist Paul Qualben writes of the three stages toward burnout, ones originally described by Cary Cherniss in *Staff Burnout:*

1. The honeymoon stage, in which enthusiasm, commitment, and job satisfaction eventually give way; energy reserves begin to drain off.

2. The "fuel shortage" stage, characterized by exhaustion, detachment, physical illness, anger, sleep disturbances, depression, possible escapist drinking or irresponsible behavior.

3. Then crisis — pessimism, self-doubt, apathy, obsession with one's own problems, disillusionment with one's career.

Stress vs. Distress

Qualben goes on to raise an intriguing question, however: "Why do some pastors . . . seem to thrive in stressful situations, find satisfaction in their work, and weather the ups and downs of personal and professional life with equanimity, while ones in the next parish burn out?" The LEADERSHIP survey responses begged the same question. Many pastors wrote that they felt positive about their ministries and couldn't imagine doing anything else; others longed to get out altogether. What set them apart?

Qualben concludes: "Most work — in the church and elsewhere — is done by people under stress. Stress is not the issue. The problem is rather distress. Distress is the product of frustration and repeated disappointment. . . . There must be other factors — within each individual — that account for the difference."[3]

Those internal factors crystallize in three personality types that Qualben identifies:

— the Type-A personalities, "hard workers who set high

goals for themselves but suffer from 'hurry disease' "
— the person who bases self-worth on the attendance, budget, and other results of ministry
— the twenty-four-hour-a-day pastor.

Pastors who tend toward these personalities are more likely to feel distress, but the three types reflect a tension felt by every minister: the tension between being a *pastor* (filling the role, performing) and being a *person* (relating to people as I am within, apart from what role I take or work I do). Most people balance the two well. In the three burnout-prone personalities, however, the individual has become always a pastor and rarely, if ever, simply a person. When he wakes up, he's a pastor; when he goes to sleep, he's a pastor; and somehow the needs of the person get squeezed out.

It's odd, but all three of these types of pastors may be getting affirmation for what they do. In fact, they're probably getting *more* affirmation than other pastors because their constant work pays off in increased visibility, higher attendance, and so on.

And yet distress sets in, because though loved for what they do, they somehow miss being loved simply for who they are. That can come, by definition, only during times of nonactivity, of rest, of refreshment. As a result, often the most "successful" are the most insecure.

The "always a pastor, never a person" syndrome traps even — perhaps especially — the most dedicated, committed, and gifted pastors. Paul Tournier, in *Escape from Loneliness*, writes: "I have rarely felt the modern man's isolation more grippingly than in a certain deaconess or pastor. Carried away in the activism rampant in the church, the latter holds meeting upon meeting, always preaching, even in personal conversation, with a program so burdened that he no longer finds time for meditation, never opening his Bible except to find subjects for his sermons. It no longer nourishes him personally. One such pastor, after several talks with me, said abruptly, 'I'm always praying as a pastor, but for a long time I've never prayed simply as a man.' "[4]

Waiting for the Soul to Catch Up

Pastors say over and over that rest — periods in which they are not "the pastor" but simply themselves — is essential.

Without that kind of rest and refreshment, the soul quickly tires. In *Springs in the Valley*, Lettie Cowman tells this story: "In the deep jungles of Africa, a traveler was making a long trek. Coolies had been engaged from a tribe to carry the loads. The first day they marched rapidly and went far. The traveler had high hopes of a speedy journey. But the second morning these jungle tribesmen refused to move. For some strange reason they just sat and rested. On inquiry as to the reason for this strange behavior, the traveler was informed that they had gone too fast the first day, and that they were now waiting for their souls to catch up with their bodies."[5]

One pastor felt the same need when she wrote on the LEADERSHIP survey: "What gives me the most discouragement is hobbies, or rather, the lack of them. I just 'veg out' on my time off; I'm so tired there's no development of an outside life." Another minister wrote that his number one struggle is finding "think time — time to meditate, to dream, to plan." Time to be a person, time for the soul to catch up — it eludes many.

Somewhere in the demanding pastoral schedule there must be a place for becoming refreshed in spirit. As important as it is to be recognized for what we do, there must be a time — regularly — for the sweeter experience of being loved just for who we are. Henri Nouwen confesses: "I'm like many pastors; I commit myself to projects and plans and then wonder how I can get them all done. This is true of the pastor, the teacher, the administrator. Indeed, it's true of our culture, which tells us, 'Do as much as you can or you'll never make it.' In that sense, pastors are part of the world. I've discovered I cannot fight the demons of busyness directly. I cannot continuously say no to this or no to that, unless there is something ten times more attractive to choose. Saying no to my lust, my greed, my needs, and the world's powers takes an enormous amount of energy.

"The only hope is to find something so obviously real and attractive that I can devote all my energies to saying yes. One such thing I can say yes to is when I come in touch with the fact that I am loved. Once I have found that in my total brokenness I am still loved, I become free from the compulsion of doing successful things."

The Problem of Prayer

Nouwen identifies the key resting place for pastors and lay people alike — in God's loving presence. As one pastor admitted, "I would have never had the inner resources to stay through the distresses that have hit my marriage, my children, and my job without finding rest in daily time alone with the Lord."

But during times of discouragement, many pastors find prayer trying and utterly unappealing. To pray seems the least likely thing to do. Finding rest and refreshment in God's presence seems unattainable.

Some pastors say that's because they feel angry at God. Admits a Midwest pastor: "When things aren't going well in ministry, I think, *Okay, God, at least show up here; let's see some fruit if we're going to put all this effort into it.* And then, just like when I get mad at my wife, I clam up. I don't talk to him."

Or prayer may become difficult because of feelings of guilt — for being discouraged, or for certain actions that have led into the discouragement. "There are times when you really don't want to go into the Lord's presence," says a Presbyterian minister, "because the light of his presence is too great."

Or prayer may simply seem futile since God, apparently, has abandoned us and disappeared. Writes Philip Yancey: "People in pain, especially those with long-term pain, often have the sensation that God has left them. No one has expressed this better than C. S. Lewis in the poignant journal he kept after his wife's death (*A Grief Observed*). He recorded that at the moment of his most profound need, God, who had seemed always available to him, suddenly seemed distant and absent, as if he had slammed a door and double-bolted it from the inside."

How have ministers — those "whose job it is to pray," Luther said — handled these periods of unappetizing prayer, and thus, been able to again find refreshment in God's presence?

"For me a big step was learning that prayer was not expressing to God the things he wanted to hear," says a Baptist minister, "but of getting honest with him — including my anger and doubt. He wasn't looking for a rote, programmed exercise but a relationship that could include all kinds of feelings." This minister goes on to admit, "I still struggle with that, though." Discouragement over their ministry, rather than becoming an unmentionable, has for some pastors become the first item on the prayer agenda.

A second realization that has helped ministers return to prayer is that "it's either pray or die," in the words of Steve Harris. "In the last couple of years it has dawned on me, *I am either going to do this or possibly lose my ministry or my marriage.* I used to give lip service to Ephesians 6:10 about spiritual warfare, and I preach about it; but I'm beginning to see that warfare is real, and prayer is therefore essential, whether I feel like doing it or not."

Another inner adjustment: recognizing, at least in their better moments, that emotional darkness and God can both be present. Indeed, the darkness may be a *sign* of his presence. "I love Francis Thompson's poem 'The Hound of Heaven,' " says Andre Bustanoby, a counselor and former pastor. "There's a line near the end where this man who is running for his life from God talks about the shadow looming over him. With a burst of insight he says, 'Is my gloom, after all, the shade of his hand outstretched caressingly?' I always think of that when I think of discouragement. There's a shadow cast over my life, but it's not the pall of doom. It's the shade of his hand outstretched caressing me. He's saying, 'My son, I'm bidding you to growth. Won't you see that as my purpose in your life?' "

In addition, many pastors have found specific methods helpful for breaking through. "My prayer life is not as vital during the times I'm discouraged," says Ed Bratcher, "but one thing that helps me is writing in my journal. My writing is for me a form of prayer: I speak about my needs and also try to express my thanksgiving for what God has done for me. I look back later and see what have been the sources of my discouragement and how some of these things have worked out. That renews me."

In Mark 2, a paralyzed man is unable to get to Jesus to be healed, so four of his friends carry him there on a stretcher. And when Jesus sees the *friends'* faith, he heals the man (Mk. 2:5). A similar principle applies to the pastor paralyzed with despondency. The only way to get to Jesus in prayer may be for friends to carry you. Robert Norris, pastor of Fourth Presbyterian Church in Bethesda, Maryland, knows what that's like. "When I don't want to pray, I get my wife to pray with me. Other times I have taken my friends and said, 'Please pray. I don't want to.' "

Those recurring battles with prayerlessness are worth fighting, report ministers who have alternately won and lost them. Writes Steve Harris: "Prayer, Bible reading, study, and meditation — though often a struggle to maintain — put us in the presence of God, and for the hurting pastor there is no better place to be."

"When I go to the Lord, I never walk away discouraged," testifies Frank Mercadante of St. John Newman Church in St. Charles, Illinois. "It's gotten now that sometimes I almost look forward to getting down, because I know that will force me to go to prayer. I might start out praying, 'Lord, this situation really stinks,' but then I begin to listen, and during that listening time I get reassured of my sonship, the Lord's call — all the things I need to hear."

It's profound, I think, that the book of the Bible that deals most directly with suffering and pain and discouragement and doubt — the Book of Job — does not provide any real "answers" to Job's dilemma. When God speaks to Job, after a thirty-seven-chapter silence, he gives not one explanation of why Job has been so afflicted. He simply reveals himself.

Yet Job found that more than enough.

So have spiritual leaders since then. As Leith Anderson, pastor of Wooddale Church in Eden Prairie, Minnesota, expressed in a recent sermon: "We say to God, 'Lord, what am I going to do about my problem?' He says, 'I am the Lord.' You say, 'But God, my situation is absolutely impossible.' He says, 'I am the Lord.' . . . We offer our problems, and he offers us himself. That is not a second-rate answer. That is the best answer that possibly could be given."[6]

No Place Like Home

In addition to the daily means of grace — prayer, Scripture reading, and other disciplines — family and vacations are other resting places for pastors, according to the LEADERSHIP survey. Pastors listed as leading encouragers *my spouse* and *my family*. Family and spouse: these are the people who accept us for who we are, not what we do. On a job interview once, I was asked, "What do you appreciate most about your family?" The question caught me by surprise, but I agree still with my answer: "When I come home, they don't care about whether I can write or edit. They just want me to be me. There's something pure in that that refreshes me."

The LEADERSHIP survey asked, "What resources does a pastor have for staying power?" to which one pastor replied, "The love and 'prejudiced' support of my wife." Spouses and family encourage us when we think we've failed, as Chuck Smith, Jr., pastor of Calvary Chapel of Dana Point (California), discovered: "One Sunday after the service, I came in and stood in the kitchen next to Chris and said, 'Can I help you with anything?' She got me busy with some vegetables, and I said, 'Boy, I just don't know about today.'

" 'What are you talking about?' she asked.

" 'Oh, the message.'

" 'Honey, it was great!' she said. 'It spoke to my needs. It was really powerful.'

" 'Thanks, Dear.'

"Then she said, 'Is that what you were fishing for?' "

That's the kind of support pastors need; it's what one writer meant when he said, "A friend is someone who, when you fail, doesn't think it's a permanent condition."

So often, had it not been for a spouse's encouragement, a pastor might have left the ministry. Recalled one pastor: "On one of those days when nothing was working and I was out of control, my wife said, 'Remember when we were zealous students attending those great rallies and would sing with much feeling, 'I'll go where you want me to go, dear Lord'?"

" 'Yeah.'

" 'Well,' she said, 'here we are! This is where he wanted us to go.'

"I was instantly healed of my frustration."

Spouses also have a wonderful way of keeping us from doing things we'd regret later. One pastor wrote of a time when he transferred his denominational affiliation and "those who supposedly loved me dropped me like a hot potato. My Navy language nearly came out several times. But Lena, my wife, restrained me from writing nasty letters. I went to prayer and confessed my wanting to return evil for evil. Lena's prayers, love, and caring through the Holy Spirit won the day."

But of all the things spouses and family do, the biggest is simply loving us as we are. James Stobaugh, pastor of Pittsburgh's Fourth Presbyterian Church, writes of his wife, Karen: "God knows we need to work on our relationship more. But I discovered seven years into our marriage that she loves me. Really loves me. In fact, I am convinced that she will always love me. That profound but simple fact of unconditional love has transformed my life. We pray together. We communicate. We face the terrors in our lives and our pasts together."

The Time Tussle

Though spouse and family were easily pastors' greatest encouragers, the third leading discourager was "lack of time with family." It's ironic: the very thing that's needed most is often the hardest to come by.

Gary Downing, executive minister of Colonial Church of Edina, Minnesota, speaks of the difficulty: "My family is both the greatest source of encouragement in my life and the greatest source of stress. The stress comes with the time issue. I'm digging a hole in the sand of community or parish needs, but I desire to be with my family. You and they both know that's the way it's got to be sometimes, but you never get to the point of liking it."

The "time issue" is a continuing battle, and a fierce one, for it's not just a matter of work versus family, but family versus family. Explains Presbyterian pastor Robert Hudnut in his book *This People, This Parish:* "One becomes close to a large number of people. Their joys become the pastor's joys. So do their sorrows. Before long the pastor feels pulled between family and church-family. Both need attention. Both are in need day and night. . . .

"The doctor or dentist or lawyer or accountant or mechanic goes home from patients, clients, or customers. The pastor goes home from brothers and sisters in Christ. They are intense competition for sons and daughters and spouse."[7]

How have ministers been able to balance church and family? What ways have they discovered to maintain their family, to nurture them and be nurtured by them? Here's their counsel.

Family Fuel

One suggestion may seem obvious, but it's often elusive: *Explain how you're feeling.* When you come home burdened about something in the ministry, it's tempting to think, *I don't want to dump my frustrations about the ministry on my wife. Now that I'm home, I want to give to her.* And there's truth in that; it's wisdom to know when and how much to share with a spouse. But many pastors have found help —and helped their spouses — by being willing to give them fair warning of their internal condition. Says John Yates: "When I'm going early morning, late night, all day in between, and not getting enough sleep, I get on edge; things get to me more. I've learned to say to my wife, 'Honey, I am really tired. And I'm really overwhelmed by this problem. I don't feel very affectionate. I want you to know I love you with all my heart and I'm committed to you and devoted to you. But I'm really irritable, so if I don't respond in the way you expect me to, please understand this is why.'

"For years, I would not be very easy to live with on Saturday nights. And she never understood it was because I was burdened about my sermon on Sunday. But one time I said, 'You know, I'm really burdened about preaching tomorrow. I don't feel ready. I don't feel it's very good. You just need to know I always get like this.' She said, 'Boy, I've never quite understood that. I'm glad you told me.' "

Block out family "appointments." One pastor learned this lesson when his secretary buzzed him and said his three o'clock appointment was there to see him — and in walked his wife. Unless we consciously designate time on the calendar for family, they won't get it. There will always be more work to do, and always "banquets and gatherings and conferences, and they are all good and all important" says Ivan York, pastor of the Wheaton (Illinois) Evangelical Free Church. "You just have to develop the ability to say no and to choose very selectively those things that you are going to be a part of." Or, as Robert Hudnut puts it, a minister must learn to "cut one's own family into one's schedule with a blowtorch."[8]

Many pastors have used the system of breaking each day into three segments — morning, afternoon, and evening — and giving one of them to family. But many arrangements are possible; a Lutheran pastor I know blocks out an extended "breakfast meeting" each week with his wife. Another pastor has involved his family in many facets of the ministry, adding to their time together by serving the church as a team.

Realize you'll always struggle to balance family and ministry was the counsel of pastors who've been around for a while. An East Coast pastor told this story: "A long time ago I ran into an older pastor at a wedding reception. He had a wonderful family, and I said, 'John, you seem to do a great job in your ministry in every way. Your family life seems to be great. How do you do it all?' He said, 'The first thing to realize is that you can't ever do it all. I don't ever remember a time in my life when my family life has been all I thought it ought to be and my ministry was all that it ought to be.'

"I can't tell you the relief that was to hear an older pastor say that," this pastor continued. "I'd always felt guilty that if my ministry was really going, I was neglecting my family. But his comment helped me realize this is an imperfect world and my wife is never going to be thoroughly satisfied with the amount of time we're having together, the communication, the camaraderie. And my desk is never going to be completely cleared off. It's just not going to ever happen.

"So you have to live in a state of tension. And it's hard and I don't like it. But I've accepted it now."

Vital Vacations

Another pastoral refresher, ranked close behind spouse and family, was *vacations*. Sometimes ministers feel like Linus when he said of his security blanket, "Only one yard of outing flannel stands between me and a nervous breakdown." Then it's time for taking a break, doing something different, getting rest.

The problem with vacations is they come but four (or two or three) weeks a year. There are long stretches, sometimes gray ones, in between. That's why I've found Tim Hansel's thinking about vacations helpful. In *When I Relax I Feel Guilty*, he describes not one kind of vacation but five.

First there is the *super-maxi vacation* — a sabbatical, a vacation coupled with conference time, or some other break from ministry that's longer than the standard vacation.

The *maxi-vacation* is what most of us think of when we hear the word *vacation* — the standard one-week or two-week trip or period of time off.

The *mini-vacation* is Hansel's term for one sabbath day per week. But there are still two more types of vacations.

"Midget vacations," Hansel writes, "fall along the same idea, but take even less time. We're called not only to structure sufficient time into each week for rest, recreation, and worship — but also into each day. Jim Carlson recently shared with me his idea for 'a daily sabbath.' He said that if we're to tithe 10 percent of our energy and finances to the Lord, then shouldn't we do it with our time as well? Basically he said that 10 percent of each day would be 2.4 hours — and he's trying to develop the discipline that will allow him to creatively dedicate that time to knowing and enjoying God more."

Hansel offers many suggestions for midget vacations. Among them:

• "Do something special for yourself in the morning —make yourself a special cup of tea, kiss your wife, pat your dog, read a favorite section of Scripture. In other words, help yourself set the pace for the day.

• "Choose one word or one line of Scripture and follow it for the day.

• "Thank someone who works at your office, or who services your home, for contributing to your life. For example, thank that secretary who answers all the phone calls."

Finally, the *minute vacation* — a sixty-second "pause that refreshes" during the day. Says Hansel: "Odd pieces of time occur everywhere, like little jewels scattered throughout your day. What about those minutes before dinner? Ever thought of taking a photo from the evening paper and asking your six-year-old to try to guess 'what's going on here?'

"What about short readings from a book of poems, or a special verse from the Book itself? Minute vacations are the time of quiet miracles."[9]

We're all well acquainted with the maxi-vacation and the mini-vacation. The other three, however, at first seem either odd or completely out of reach. But they are possible. Many pastors told me of the refreshment and staying power they'd found through broadening their vacation repertoire to include midget vacations, minute vacations, and yes, even the super-maxi sabbatical.

Midget and Minute Vacations

The secret of the midget vacation is that *doing* something, be it ever so small, is critical for refreshment. Most of us, when we're discouraged, want to sit and think about it, to stew in it. Fred Smith, a Dallas business executive, describes the problem: "I've found a sure cure for mild depression and a guarantee for its continuation. The guarantee for its continuation is inactivity. The sure cure for its cessation is activity. If I feel the least bit depressed, I don't dare sit and meditate, although I'm always tempted to meditate my way out of depression. That's as impossible as Joseph trying to meditate his way out of the bedroom of Potiphar's wife. Certain things just do not go together. Meditating your way out of depression doesn't work.

"If I immediately get busy, particularly with something that makes me physically tired — something that I enjoy doing —I find any kind of *mild* depression will leave. You've got to use your will power in various ways to change unhealthy stress."

One question on the LEADERSHIP survey asked, "What kinds of things refresh you and keep you going during down times in ministry?" Many of the responses qualify as midget or minute vacations. Each is a short, relatively inexpensive, and surprisingly refreshing way pastors have used to deal with mild discouragement:

- shutting myself in my home and listening to sacred music
- playing basketball at the YMCA
- reading great preachers of the past
- working around the home
- wearing blue jeans. Whenever I can, it is just like a day off!

- jogging
- having a guest preacher so I get a Sunday out of the pulpit
- reading over notes of encouragement I've saved.

One pastor often drives an hour to a place in the country on Fridays. "I've found I need it personally in a way I never understood. About the time I get halfway out there, it's as though everything just kind of melts off my shoulders and I begin to sing and praise the Lord. I can go out there and just stay an hour and come back so refreshed. It changes my perspective. I come back thinking, *Well, that problem's probably not as big a deal as I felt it was.*"

Super-maxi Vacations

Many pastors have found a super-maxi vacation possible through a trip to the Holy Land. "We took about forty people from church and were gone for a couple of weeks," says a Virginia pastor. "That was so much fun. It was so great to have two weeks together with forty folks in the church, to study Scripture together, to act out Bible stories at those key sites. I had no idea that would be such a refreshing, encouraging time. And I really saw people grow during that time."

But the ultimate — usually pronounced "unheard-of" — dream for pastors is a sabbatical. "I can't believe I did it," admits Eugene Peterson. "About two or three years ago I began feeling tired. I was wearing down. I'd always wanted to stay here, but I didn't want to be less than my best here.

"So I started thinking, *What can I do?* The obvious thing was to change churches, but I didn't want to do that if I could help it. I thought and I prayed and all of a sudden I thought, *Why not a sabbatical?* The problem was this is a small parish. They can't afford to do that."

But gradually, over the next year or so, pieces began to fall into place: an intern to handle the pastoral duties, a generous gift from a friend, a creative housing arrangement. After twenty-three years in the same parish, a dream came true.

The results? "I feel like I've got the energy of a fifteen-year-old again. I have embraced parts of ministry I used to avoid and found grace there; it has surprised the socks off me. Everyone has noticed a big difference in me since I've been back."

But is it *really* possible? "Pastors get no encouragement for it," Eugene admits. And for some, such an extended break may not be feasible. But his experience — and others' —shows that for many pastors, even those who'd never thought it possible, it can be done.

"I have a friend, the pastor of a little church in Victor, Montana, who's about thirty-three," Eugene says. "He said to his congregation, 'In ten years, I want to go to Germany for a year and study at the University of Hamburg. Would you help me?'

"Here's a little church — a yoked parish, actually. But they're used to having pastors every two or three years. So when he said, 'I don't want to move. I want to pastor here. But I think I'm going to need some help,' they were delighted to think the pastor would be with them for ten years and then even come back and still be their pastor. They could hardly believe that anybody would care for them that much, and so every year now they're setting money aside so that in ten years he and his wife can go to Germany."

Going Guilty, Coming Back Calm

For some of us, the tough hurdle in taking a break or being with family is not so much the external difficulties of making sure things will be taken care of while we're gone, but the internal difficulty of guilt. We think of the desk not cleared, the phone messages yet to return, the people we really ought to visit, and then we hear in our conscience the words of Charles Spurgeon: "The man who does not make hard work of his ministry will find it very hard work to answer for his idleness at the last great day."

But great work, fruitful work, comes only through rest and refreshment.

It may seem, when we head for the YMCA, the retreat center, the restaurant, that we are wasting time; it's tempting to think how much we could be doing if we weren't sitting at our son's baseball game. But when we've spent time with our God and our family and our friends simply as a person — and been loved — we return with an inner vitality that not only fuels our work but is our work.

I shudder when I read of the tireless output of John Wesley, who during his fifty-two years of itinerant ministry traveled 208,000 miles — most of them on foot or horseback — and preached some 40,000 sermons. But Wesley knew a secret: "Though I am always in haste, I am never in a hurry because I never undertake more work than I can go through with calmness of spirit." Wesley knew of rest and refreshment.

---

1. Tim Hansel, *When I Relax I Feel Guilty* (Elgin, Ill.: David C. Cook, 1979), 20 – 21.
2. Laura Deming and Jack Stubbs, *Men Married to Ministers* (Washington, D.C.: Alban Institute).
3. Paul A. Qualben, "A Cool Look at Burning Out," *LCA Partners* (December 1982).
4. Cited by James L. Johnson, "The Ministry Can Be Hazardous to Your Health," *Leadership* (Winter 1980), 26 – 27.
5. Cited by Gordon MacDonald, *Restoring Your Spiritual Passion* (Nashville: Thomas Nelson, 1986).
6. Leith Anderson, "Unlistened-to Lessons of Life," *Preaching Today* (48, August 1987), audiotape.
7. Robert Hudnut, *This People, This Parish* (Grand Rapids, Mich.: Zondervan, 1986).
8. Ibid.
9. Hansel, 125 – 39.

NINE

CAN I PREDICT WHEN DOWN TIMES ARE GOING TO HIT?

If the owner of the house had known at what time of night the thief was coming, he would have kept watch and would not have let his house be broken into. So you also must be ready.

JESUS (Matthew 24:43-44a)

T

hey say pro football quarterbacks fear one thing almost more than anything else: being blind-sided.

When you take the snap and drop back into the pocket, you become a tasty morsel dangling in front of hungry defensive ends and blitzing middle linebackers. These wolves weigh 265 pounds apiece and can sprint the distance between the line and your tender body in two seconds flat. Their trip to the Pro Bowl depends on how many times they can slam you to the Astroturf.

But as long as you can see them coming, you're pretty safe. You can dodge; you can duck, scramble, get a pass off, or head for the sidelines. Roger Staubach, the former Dallas Cowboys great, describes the dynamic in a play against the Los Angeles Rams in the early seventies: "I took the snap, dropping back to pass. A defensive lineman broke loose on my left. I ducked and he went over me. I rolled to my left and Mike Montgomery, sensing that I might run, knocked down the linebacker on that side, Isiah Robertson. I took off for the first down."[1]

It's when you can't see them coming that there's trouble. You cock your arm to throw, you're concentrating only on that tight end cutting across midfield, and WHAM! Your head snaps back, and the wind's knocked out of you. Then you crunch the turf.

The situation's not too different for pastors trying to dodge discouragement. If only you could learn to read when discouragement might come at you, you could keep from getting blindsided.

Reading the Blitz

I asked veteran pastors who have learned to "read the blitz" when discouragement and down times were most likely to come.

The first key time, oddly, is following a big event, a major victory. D. Martyn Lloyd-Jones, the brilliant preacher at London's Westminster Chapel earlier this century, explains: "Another frequent cause of spiritual depression is what we may describe as a reaction — a reaction after a great blessing, a reaction after some unusual and exceptional experience. Consder the case of Elijah under the juniper tree. There is no doubt in my mind that his main trouble was he was suffering from a reaction after what had happened on Mount Carmel (1 Kings 19)."[2] The great prophet had called down fire from heaven to display dramatically that Jehovah, not Baal, is the one true God; yet scant verses later he is in the throes of depression and self-pity. Valley follows mountaintop.

What happened to Elijah happens also to spiritual leaders today. "One time when I'm vulnerable to discouragement," reflects a Baptist pastor, "is following big events such as weddings and funerals. After a week of being up I've found I crash, sometimes for three days. I try to think about why I'm discouraged, and there's no apparent reason. Then I look at my previous week's schedule, and I think, *Of course you're discouraged. Look what you've been through.*"

Says another church leader, "I've learned simply to look at my schedule when I'm down. Blue days invariably follow my periods of most intense activity. Now I try to plan days of rest to recuperate."

But many ministers say they struggle to accept the fact that they have good reason to be discouraged. Confesses one: "I don't consciously think that way. Instead I think, *What's wrong with me? I shouldn't be down. I just had a great week — a top-of-the-mountain challenge. Besides, I'm a leader. I should be able to forge ahead.*"

But the fact is, following a big event most people experience a drop of adrenalin. An emotional drop is the natural accompaniment.

This principle helps us to interpret down times not solely as indictments of our own spirituality or character. It helps us put them in perspective. These down times following a major success or goal reached may be the most normal possible reaction. That knowledge brings some comfort; it keeps us, as Presbyterian minister Bruce Thielemann put it, from "adding to the weight of discouragement the burden of blame."

Weak During the Week

Discouragement also comes at predictable moments during the week, according to many pastors. "After Sunday's service is the worst time," says Robert Norris. "You begin to say to yourself, *Everything I've done is in vain. Who was helped?*" So much emotional energy has been expended in the preparation and delivery of a message that following this high point, optimism and energy drop off.

Often the emotions fully bottom out on Monday. "In my first pastorate, I would be really irritable and grumpy every Monday," says Glen Parkinson, minister at Severna Park (Maryland) Presbyterian Church. "That was my day off, so it ended up being the day when my wife and I would have our fights. It would be just terrible.

"After four years of that somebody told me, 'That's no big surprise. Look at what you do on Sunday. It isn't the amount of work; it's what you put into it. And preaching is a very emotional thing. Of course you are going to drop!'

"Well, the next week I got up on Monday morning, and I felt terrible. But it wasn't so bad because I thought, *Of course I feel terrible. That's okay. I don't have to get mad at anybody.* It was wonderful."

Recognizing this, some ministers have switched their day off to some day other than Monday so their spouses and family don't get them at their worst. They use Monday to catch up on light office work. As one minister quipped, "Hey, if you're going to have an off day, do it on company time." One who made the switch was Steve Harris. His evaluation: "I take Thursdays off now, and though it seems like a small thing, it has made the rhythm of the week much better. Sunday used to be the end of the week, and I'd think, *If I can just get through the day, I'll be off tomorrow.* But when I take Thursday off, I hit my peak around Sunday."

But again, a low period during the week signals nothing more than normalcy. Recognizing that has given Phil Sackett, pastor of Excelsior (Minnesota) Bible Church, staying power. "I've made a deal with the Lord," he says, "never to quit on a Monday or the day after a board meeting. Anything I do has to be thought out longer than that."

Weathering the Year

With that kind of weekly cycle, pastors can expect, in the words of veteran Methodist minister Phil Hinerman, "some mornings each month when I feel like nobody loves me and nobody cares about me. So I just get up and go to work and believe the feeling will pass."

Lows cycle through the year as well, usually following the "right after highs" pattern. "A couple of weeks before Labor Day you really start cranking," says Chuck Smalley, associate pastor of Wayzata (Minnesota) Evangelical Free Church. "You start all the new small groups, hold a couple of conferences or retreats — from Labor Day to Thanksgiving you run full blast.

"Then in November you usually bottom out emotionally because you've gone through that intense period. And here in Minnesota, November is the pits for weather — brown, cold, muddy, yuck. All the leaves are gone, but the snow hasn't come yet.

"The other time I tend to get low during the year is right after all the activities leading up to, and around, Easter. Now that I've identified the cycle, I just plan to take a couple of days off at those points."

Chuck's description raises another factor in the yearly cycle: the weather. There's good reason why people often describe times of discouragement as gray, cold, or rainy. A real estate agent once told me, "If you can love a house in November or February, you really love it." And the same applies to churches: If you can feel positive about your ministry in November or February, that's a good sign. In the last few years researchers have documented an intriguing depression they call *SAD* (Seasonal Affective Disorder), which strikes certain people only during the winter months. Not that cold, short days are the major factor in pastoral discouragement, but it helps to keep in mind the counsel of Bruce Chapman, pastor of First Evangelical Free Church in Minneapolis: "I had a denominational leader tell me, 'In Minnesota, never make a decision in February.' He wasn't being sarcastic. And I agree. Don't make a major decision when you're feeling down."

Career Culverts

Even more helpful is asking the long-range question: Across my entire ministry, when am I most likely to get discouraged? What ages and stages in ministry make me prone to it?

Church consultant Robert Dale identified three times in the pastor's life when difficulties may become insurmountable:
• three to five years out of seminary
• around age forty
• near retirement.
These three career culverts bear a closer look.

Three to five years into ministry. The feeling of fading ideals was captured by one fifth-year pastor in a letter to a friend at the same point in ministry: "Early in my first pastorate, I remember my wife and me visiting our hometown and going to the church pastored by the man who married us. After the service, we greeted him and said how great it was to be in the ministry. I expected him to agree it was a great calling and that he was enjoying it just as much after twenty years in the pastorate.

"He shocked us both by saying he was glad we were enjoying it, but for him the ministry was full of heartache and pain. I quickly chalked it up to his carnality and obvious disregard for the calling he had received.

"But now, five years later, I know what he was talking about. I've come face to face with the pain of pastoring. I've watched myself become depressive, moody, impatient with my children, impatient with my church. It doesn't take much to put me in a tailspin over some real or imagined slight. I know I'm not God's gift to the church, but some people in the congregation seem to feel it's their duty before God to question everything I do."

A LEADERSHIP Journal study a few years ago isolated the factors that increase the chances of emotional problems for pastors. One of the top factors was shortness of time in the pastorate. First churches often aren't everything a pastor hoped for. Then, a young pastor faces each problem for the first time ever. It's no wonder seminary-bred ideals soon get pricked on the barbed-wire realities of a local church.

But another troubling factor, the study found, was shortness of time in the current position. The "at-three-to-five-years" discouragement, according to many pastors, comes not only in your first church, but in each church. Lynn Anderson, who has ministered at the Highland Church of Christ in Abilene, Texas for the past sixteen years, sketches the period this way:

"The first two years you can do nothing wrong.

"The second two years you can do nothing right.

"The fifth and sixth years of a ministry, either you leave or the people who think you can do nothing right leave. Or you change, or they change, or you both change.

"Productive ministry emerges somewhere in the seventh year or beyond."

What's behind the three-to-five-year problem?

"By then," explains veteran pastor Ivan York of the Wheaton (Illinois) Evangelical Free Church, "you start to realize idiosyncrasies of your church that you couldn't see when you first arrived. They are starting to see some of the imperfections in you. They knew all along you weren't a superhero, yet they were daring to hope — until now."

A pastor from the East who survived such a period described it this way: "When I came, they said they wanted renewal, outreach, evangelism, and all this stuff. But their understanding of what that meant and mine weren't the same. In the first three or four years, I kept having encounters with people who had been close to the former pastor, people who in my opinion had deep insecurities and personal problems. They were not people I would ever bring into the inner circle of my ministry. I guess they sensed that and resented it.

"As a result, they accused me of being anti-intellectual, on an ego trip — that I was building my own kingdom. One man, who was an elected member of our leadership, finally resigned and wrote a four-page, single-spaced letter questioning my motives and competence. That was a discouraging time."

Carl George, director of the Charles E. Fuller Institute of Church Growth, pinpoints the sociological factors that troubled these, and many other, pastors. The first is that usually at about four years in a new ministry, the new guard — those members who have come *since* the pastor, and largely because of him or her — "nears equality with the old guard in voting power, and the old guard often feels threatened.

"Second, some time after four years, a congregation begins to realize the minister's agenda for the future may contradict some of the long-established members' agendas. This period of delicate balance commonly takes place between the fourth and sixth years of a given pastorate.

"The pastor enjoys little security through this period. In fact, the pastor fatality rate at this time is so high that whole denominations have that 'about four years' pattern for pastorates."

Recognizing that may not make the difficulties easier, but it does provide the comfort that the problems are not unusual, not an indication of lack of ministerial gifts.

Midlife adds a new element to a pastor's outlook on ministry: there's not all that much time left. Earlier lifetime goals may suddenly, and painfully, have to be revised. Many middle-aged pastors feel they'd like to try something new, take on a new church, give one more great push in their lives before time runs out. But the realistic options may be few. Lamented one pastor on the LEADERSHIP survey: "I have feelings of futility, but I'm financially trapped. Middle-aged expositors are not in great demand."

Early in ministry, they could try new things, tackle challenges, and if the thing blew up — well, they'd just start over. There was plenty of time to learn and give it another shot.

But not so now. Psychiatrist Louis McBurney, who counsels many pastors, capsulizes the pressured feeling: "They're no longer able to bounce back from disappointments."

When discouragement hits at midlife, it often comes as a complex tangle of situations and feelings. Because of that, it may well require new coping strategies, ones a pastor had not considered seriously before, as Ed Bratcher found. "Without question, the period in my ministry when I felt the greatest discouragement was right around age forty. The despondency over my ministry coincided with some personal factors. My father died. My mother came to live with us and brought the new dynamic of three generations under one roof.

"I began to feel, because of my age, that I was trapped. I wondered if my mobility had stopped, if there was no place to go. My discouragement sank into a clinically discernible depression, and when I saw a physician, he asked me, 'You wouldn't consider getting professional help, would you?' My stance at the time was a firm no, but I was depressed enough that I really did need some professional help."

Ed eventually overcame his apprehension that parishioners might find out and react negatively to the fact their pastor had sought psychiatric help. His experience? "I can testify to both the fears and the benefits of receiving psychiatric help. Even though I still find it difficult to admit to members of my parish that my wife and I have had psychiatric care, I can acknowledge the value of such care. My ministry through interpersonal relationships has become more sensitive and of greater benefit to everyone involved as a result of the psychiatric help I've received."[3]

Knowing when and how to get help is one of the great secrets of staying power for the discouraged pastor, and that may be especially true for the pastor wrestling with midlife questions of self-worth, achievement, and the future.

Nearing retirement. Later in life people hit a psycho-social stage that noted researcher Erik Erikson characterized as "Integrity versus Despair." The pastor headed toward retirement takes stock of his ministry and wonders, *Did I do well? Can I rejoice that I accomplished things, that my life and work had a wholeness and integrity? Or do I look back and only despair?*

The turning point in the decision is often whether a pastor can see progress. Did people really change? Were new leaders developed? Did the church grow? Were buildings added? Where there is a sense of progress made, there is usually a sense of integrity as well. One minister, now in retirement, wrote: "It seems to me that the whole of my life as a pastor has offered the kind of affirmation that made me want to stay in ministry. Really, it has been a joy with few down moments, even when dealing with a bishop who seemed to me unreasonable and plain ornery. I enjoy reflecting on my years in ministry." This pastor adds that he is "still at it, even in retirement."

For others, though, who see primarily blocked progress

and unrealized dreams as they look back, discouragement can hit hard. "The older I get in ministry, the easier it is to feel discouraged," admits one minister. "You see the same thing coming time upon time, and there doesn't seem to be any change."

Preparation for Protection

Knowing that at these times the tide of discouragement will be coming in and the waves may be high, can pastors prepare themselves? Are there ways to brace yourself for the waves? Ministers I talked with described two ways they prepare themselves.

Take a firm footing in God. "The way I prepare myself for dark times," says Dave Dorpat, pastor of Faith Lutheran Church in Geneva, Illinois, "is to get my relationship with the Lord in order. When that's solid, I know I'm on the Rock, and like the Psalmist says, 'Ten thousand may fall at my right or left, but the Lord is with me.' "

"You can prepare yourself by building spiritual disciplines," adds Frank Mercadante, youth minister at a large church in nearby St. Charles, Illinois. "When I've been spending time with the Lord and the tough times come, they're still tough, but I have a foundation of my relationship with him, and I can rely on that rather than on myself."

Frank discovered this once after a program he'd long dreamed of didn't gain the necessary approval and funding. "That really hurt," he says, "but as I prayed about it the Lord said to me, 'Frank, there's nothing that can hold back my will. You're disappointed now, but I'm God and you're the servant. Don't worry; I'm in control.' And that gave me the strength to go on."

Find firm friends. The second thing pastors have found helpful is "gathering a group who will care for you amidst discouragement," as one put it. "You have to assemble those people who will gather around you, support you, maintain you."

"I can't overemphasize my need to have leaders whom I

relate to and spend time with, people who will pray with me and support me," adds Dave Dorpat.

"Recently, for instance, I have been helping take care of my father-in-law, who has a broken hip, at nights, so my mother-in-law can get some sleep. Being there every night for the last two weeks and having my sleep interrupted has really been wearing on me. By last Sunday when I came to church, I was wiped out. I was really empty. I didn't have a conclusion for the message; I just didn't know what I was going to say.

"We have prayer at 7:15 before the services, and one of our elders, Dean Kroning, came bounding in all joyous and praising the Lord. So I said, 'You know, I feel really tired this morning. Wiped out. Empty. Could you pray for me?' And Dean and the four or five other elders who were there gathered around, laid hands on me, and prayed for me. And the message that morning — well, I think the Lord really blessed it. Several people told me it was powerful."

These people lift your sights. They remind you of the things you easily forget when you're down — that God is in control, that he loves you, that he's working in your life. Right now, to use the football metaphor, discouragement may be blitzing, but friends block for you. They keep you playing toward your ultimate goal.

In his autobiography, Roger Staubach tells of the time he was asked by a reporter, "What's your ultimate goal in life?"

"My ultimate goal is beyond this life," Staubach told him. "It's going to heaven." Then he added, "All your passes are completed in heaven."

"What about defensive backs?" the reporter came back.

"There are no defensive backs up there."[4]

---

1. Roger Staubach with Sam Blair and Bob St.John, *Staubach: First Down, Lifetime to Go* (Waco, Tex.: Word, 1974), 250.
2. D. Martyn Lloyd-Jones, *Spiritual Depression: Its Causes and Cure* (Grand Rapids, Mich.: Eerdmans, 1973).
3. Edward B. Bratcher, *The Walk-on-Water Syndrome* (Waco, Tex.: Word, 1984), 114.
4. Staubach, 238.

IS THIS A SPIRITUAL PROBLEM?

After a spirit of discernment, the next rarest things in the world are diamonds and pearls.

BRUYERE

I never know how much of my discouragement is just low metabolism, how much of it is the attack of the Enemy, and how much of it is the sheer toughness of the job," a pastor admitted to me recently.

Are down times caused by our makeup, by the influence of evil, or by God's shaping hand? Is discouragement mostly spiritual, emotional, or physical in origin? Is it a sin we should feel bad about, or a normal human response, like grief? Is it something we need to repent of, rebuke, or just rest from?

The way we answer these questions makes an Atlantic-sized difference. The answer determines whether we will feel guilty for being discouraged — and whether that guilt is accurate. It determines whether we will seek help — and if so, where and how. It even helps determine how long we will feel discouraged, for applying the wrong treatment can be worse than doing nothing at all.

These questions don't take easy answers. Discouragement and depression, its unpleasant cousin, usually involve a complex of factors — physical, mental, emotional, spiritual, and social. Discouraged pastors report sheer fatigue, waking up tired. They also talk of not wanting to be around people, of withdrawing socially. Many lose interest in spiritual disciplines such as prayer and Bible study. A pastor feels discouragement at all levels.

But what about pinpointing the cause? H. B. London, pastor of First Church of the Nazarene in Pasadena, California, knows the importance of "trying to retrace how I'm feeling and why. If it's fatigue, then it makes sense. If it's failure, then it makes sense. Knowing the cause doesn't make the discouragement go away, but there's help in being able to say, 'Hey, I'm really tired,' or 'I blew it. That was a lousy sermon and I know it; it doesn't matter what anybody else says, I know it was a lousy sermon.' Or if I can trace my feelings to family problems or finances, then I at least have a reason for what's bothering me and can work on it."

Diagnosing Discouragement

One way pastors have tried to analyze their discouragement is to determine whether it's primarily physical, emotional, or spiritual in nature.

Physical. "I can see a pattern in the things that bring me down," one minister says, "and it's this: Physical tiredness relates directly to discouragement in ministry."

For spiritual leaders trained in the ways of prayer and spiritual vitality, it's easy to chalk up much if not all of the discouragement we feel to spiritual problems — *I haven't prayed enough; I'm growing cold; the Lord is dealing with me.*

But more often than we suspect, as Martyn Lloyd-Jones wrote in *Spiritual Depression: Its Causes and Cure,* "Physical conditions play their part. Certain physical ailments tend to promote depression. . . . Take that great preacher who preached in London for nearly forty years in the last century, Charles Spurgeon. He was subject to spiritual depression, and the main explanation in his case was undoubtedly the fact that he suffered from a gouty condition which finally killed him. He had to face this problem of spiritual depression often in a most acute form. A tendency to acute depression is an unfailing accompaniment of the gout he inherited from his forebears."[1]

Many of the physical connections to discouragement are not yet known, but plenty are, and most of these can be controlled. For example, pastors generally work long hours, get little rest, and have trouble finding time to exercise. Unchecked, that pattern will almost surely lead to discouragement.

Experienced ministers have learned that it pays to not neglect their rest, relaxation, exercise, and proper diet. The body is probably the most easily overlooked source of discouragement — but often it's a significant one.

Emotional and social causes may be easiest to pinpoint as causes of discouragement. Most of the cries discussed in chapters 4–8, for example, center in these areas. *I can't use my gifts, I need affirmation* — these reflect emotional and social needs that, when unmet, can bring discouragement.

In addition, though, the pastorate tends to promote loneliness, as any leadership position does. Ironically pastors may be constantly contacting people, yet face, as Calvin Miller wrote, "lonely nights that follow the hectic days when it seems that, for all my acquaintances, I haven't got a friend in the world." The problem is not the number of contacts but the nature of them. Unless some are the refreshing personal kind, where a pastor can truly express his or her feelings, loneliness may dog even the most people-oriented pastor.

When social and emotional pressures build, the temptation may be to cloister yourself, to pray and study, to stay where it's safe. But "it is a psychological fact that one cannot resolve conflicts or clarify issues simply by thinking about them," says Arch Hart in his helpful book *Coping with Depression in the Ministry and Other Helping Professions.* "Self-talk and introspective rumination with no outside input leads inevitably to distortion and irrationality, whereas talking things over with someone else can help to clarify issues and remove distortions."[2]

When discouraged by emotional or social conflicts or difficulties, the natural response is withdrawal. Yet unless there's some social interaction, the problem becomes nearly impossible to trace.

Spiritual. Most pastors have sensitive antennae to the spiritual causes of their discouragement. As an Illinois pastor described it: "My discouragement is directly linked to my spiritual life. If I don't have a strong spiritual life, if my prayer life is inconsistent, it's easy for me to get down. I know that burnout and discouragement can happen even with a strong spiritual life, but I do think that encompasses a big part of it."

During down times, many ministers feel as Spurgeon felt: "I fear I am not so full of love to God as I used to be. I lament my sad decline in spiritual things. . . . What is it to be popular, to be successful, to have abundance — if I should be left of God to fall, and to depart from his ways?"

But the temptation during times of discouragement is to place the blame wholly there. Then we either withdraw further from the Lord, out of guilt, or throw ourselves utterly into spiritual disciplines. While prayer is always helpful, too much seclusion for the discouraged person can bring on further heaviness of heart. Teresa of Avila spoke of the potential danger: "Let not your soul coop itself up in a corner. In attaining to great sanctity in . . . seclusion, the devil will keep you company there. And so he will do your sequestered soul much mischief."

Here many pastors stressed the importance of a spiritual confidant to help them stay spiritually vital and discern more accurately the spiritual causes, if any, of their discouragement. Delbert Rossin, pastor of Faith Lutheran Church in Geneva, Illinois, is one who has experienced the benefit of such a person. "It is pretty hard sometimes all by yourself. I think we all need pastors, spiritual advisers. I'm on the phone to my pastor in Minneapolis once a month, and I ask him to hold me accountable — am I growing in the Lord? He holds me accountable in a loving way; it's not legalistic. I was going through a time when my Bible reading and prayer time was less than it ought to be — not that we ever arrive. My pastor said to me, 'Del, why don't you try this: no Bible, no breakfast.' That little routine has helped keep me more faithful and disciplined in this area. On my own, it wouldn't do any good. But knowing he supports me, is praying for me, and that he wonders how it's going keeps me motivated."

Mapping Spiritual Pain

Even when we accurately trace our discouragement to the spiritual area of life, we may not yet have pinpointed the precise cause. For within the spiritual realm — a complex and invisible one — several things may cause discouragement, according to pastors.

Basic weariness of the human spirit. One leader described discouragement this way: "It goes deeper than stress or burnout. It's when the whole spirit just sags." Counselor G. Keith Olson has pointed out that "the greatest enemy of parents is discouragement," and the same holds true for spiritual parents. There is great agony in bringing flawed human beings into the image of Christ. It was for good reason that Paul wrote, "I'm in labor again until Christ is formed in you!" One pastor wrote on the LEADERSHIP survey, "My greatest sense of discouragement comes from dealing with the marital and emotional and spiritual problems of new converts." When you've invested yourself heavily in a person, especially a young believer, you are going to feel some spiritual tiredness. Just as physical labor causes sore muscles, so spiritual labor can cause a spiritual weariness. That's why Jesus withdrew often for prayer and rest.

God's shaping hand. The mystery is great, but the unanimous testimony of church leaders through the ages is that God sometimes withdraws a sense of his presence — brings spiritual dryness — to bring growth and maturity in Christ. (Indeed, Jesus himself was "led by the Spirit" into the wilderness of temptation, Mark tells us.) Bartholomew Gottemoller, a contemporary churchman, described such a period: "For six or seven years . . . I did not know where I was spiritually since everything seemed to be going wrong. . . . All my dreams of achieving holiness looked like mere folly. Prayer became dry and difficult. Because of all this, I felt that God was displeased with me, that he had given up on me because of my many faults and failings. The best word I can find to express what I was experiencing is 'aimlessness.' I wanted to live for God because I knew he was the only real good, but I did not know how to go about it."

But then Gottemoller went on a retreat and heard expounded the "I am the vine, you are the branches" passage from John 15. He saw that "every branch that bears fruit he prunes," and something broke loose within him. "I clearly saw that it was his work and not my doing. What I had thought was actually destroying my spiritual life I now saw he had been using to bring me to a goal I could never have imagined."[3]

Spiritual discouragement may be God's tool to make us more like Christ. Oswald Chambers spoke of it in these words: "If you are going through a time of discouragement, there is a big personal enlargement ahead."[4]

Satan. C. S. Lewis wrote of the "two equal and opposite errors into which our race can fall about the devils. One is to disbelieve in their existence. The other is to believe, and to feel an excessive and unhealthy interest in them. They themselves are equally pleased by both errors and hail a materialist or a magician with equal delight."[5]

Finding that balance isn't always easy. On the one hand, as an Evangelical Free Church pastor put it, "Satan gets way too much credit for discouragement, I think. Most of the discouragement I've gone through came from my own poor performance. Here in the middle of summer, for example, I'm probably going to have to work all day tomorrow, my day off. I'm also going to have to work all afternoon and evening on Sunday. I look at that and say, 'That's discouraging.' But I recognize that's no one's fault but my own; I just didn't plan very well."

It's no less true, however, as Dallas Seminary professor Howard Hendricks says, that "when you are doing what

Jesus Christ has called you to do, you can count on two things: you will possess spiritual power because you have the presence of Christ, and you'll experience opposition."

In *Shadow of the Almighty*, Elisabeth Elliot writes of the time shortly before her husband, Jim, set out to bring the gospel to the Aucas, a hostile South American Indian tribe. "But the Enemy of Souls is not easily persuaded to relinquish his hold in any territory. Seeing that his authority in the Auca region was going to be challenged, he soon launched an attack on the challengers. Jim was beset with temptations such as had never before assailed him, and that master-weapon, discouragement, which to my knowledge had held no power over him since his arrival in Ecuador, met him at every turn. A gloom seemed to settle over his spirit in December, and it seemed that battles were being fought which I could not share."[6]

Ben Haden, pastor of First Presbyterian Church in Chattanooga, describes the same opposition this way: "The ministry is a life-and-death, heaven-or-hell matter. It's a spiritual battle every day — if you're faithful.

"I find my struggle with Satan usually occurs when I've made the gospel clear but individuals can't bring themselves to respond. They understand what I'm saying and know what is required, but as they weigh their willingness to make the commitment, it becomes obvious there's spiritual opposition. That's what I mean by spiritual warfare, and it's a draining experience."

Sifting and Sorting

"When it's happening, when you're down or discouraged, you often don't know why," admitted a Lutheran pastor. Indeed, one characteristic of discouragement is the inability to think clearly. You see the entire world through "gray-colored lenses." Gaining an objective view of the situation is difficult.

What's needed is to find out, one pastor explained, "what is the truth of the situation. Is it true, for example, that nobody likes me? You have many voices speaking to you — your own inside you, other people's, and the Devil's. But you need to hear the truth, which is God's voice."

Pastors do have some substantial resources to gain a more objective view of their situations.

One is time. During discouragement the present seems insurmountable. Even a few days down the road can help us see things more clearly. "I'll get out and run in the morning, and say to myself, *Give it seventy-two hours and then evaluate the problem*," explains Leith Anderson, pastor of Wooddale Church in Eden Prairie, Minnesota.

Another pastoral ally is rest. A day away for relaxation often puts things into perspective.

The biggest resource is often talking out the situation. Some pastors do that with a journal. Robert Frederich, pastor of Denver's Galilee Baptist Church, says, "One of the most helpful tools for me is my journal in which I begin each day by answering the question, 'Where am I?' Am I tired? Depressed? Worried? By putting it down, I can define the nebulous feelings and relate them to the resources of God."

Often it's wise to go to someone outside the situation, someone who can remind us we're loved and accepted, and who can reorient our sights. Many leaders' spouses, though not completely removed from the situation, serve that purpose. "The major problem in my life and ministry has been depression," confesses Howard Hendricks. "That will surprise even some of my closest friends, because I've tried hard to be a positive, confident person. I've come home from a week of ministry where I've been so far beyond myself it was pitiful, where God did things far beyond my own spiritual capabilities, and as soon as I hit Dallas, I was in trouble. I'd crash. I would tell my wife, 'Honey, I've had it.'

"She would say, 'Well, Hon, why don't we pray together?'

" 'No, I don't want to pray.'

" 'Why don't we read the Word together?'

" 'No, I don't want to read the Word.'

"And she just kept right on loving me and accepting me. What can you do in the face of that? You change."

Is Discouragement Sin?

You can't talk about the causes of discouragement for very long before you have to deal with a tough question head-on: Is discouragement sin?

The case for discouragement being a sin usually runs like this: Whatever is not of faith is sin, and discouragement is not of faith; instead it's a sign of unbelief. In addition, the Lord commanded Joshua (1:10) to not be discouraged, and Paul said that he did not lose heart (2 Cor. 4:1). Further, discouragement may have negative effects in our lives, such as causing us to withdraw from others or God. Thus, discouragement is sin.

One minister expressed his belief this way: "Treat discouragement as a sin and shun it."

Pastors find this line of reasoning difficult when they become discouraged from circumstances beyond their control. When a staff member resigns, pointing the finger at you, it's hard to make sin the culprit.

And yet we all know cases where people's discouragement was in some way tied to sin.

Arch Hart makes a helpful distinction "between the *causes* of depression and the *experience* of depression. The *experience* of depression is always legitimate. It is a natural and normal response to something happening either in our environment or in our bodies. The *cause* of depression may not be."[7]

It's a (Self-)Pity

In addition, though feelings of discouragement are themselves a normal response (to something out of kilter in our lives), we may sin in the way we handle those feelings once we have them. For example, rather than seek out appropriate help, we may fall into self-pity.

One Methodist minister confessed, "It's embarrassing to admit, but sometimes I actually *want* to feel sorry for myself, to feel down. I don't want help from God, my wife, or anyone else."

"Self-pity is absolutely devastating," Howard Hendricks says. "I think I've set a new record for resigning from the institution. One day my wife said, 'Honey, why don't you just write out the resignation and put it in the drawer? It will save you a lot of trouble.' "

Oswald Chambers, in his characteristically piercing prose, explains why self-pity is so destructive in the Christian life: "We think it a sign of real modesty to say at the end of a day, 'Oh, well, I have just gotten through, but it has been a severe tussle.' And all the Almighty God is ours in the Lord Jesus! And he will tax the last grain of sand and the remotest star to bless us if we will obey him. What does it matter if external circumstances are hard? Why should they not be! If we give way to self-pity and indulge in the luxury of misery, we banish God's riches from our own lives and hinder others from entering into his provision. No sin is worse than the sin of self-pity, because it obliterates God and puts self-interest upon the throne. It opens our mouths to spit out murmurings, and our lives become craving spiritual sponges; there is nothing lovely or generous about them."[8]

Pastors are unanimous in their assessment of the dangers of self-pity. It keeps us from seeking help, it keeps us from shaking off our discouragement when that's possible, and it keeps us from responding to God during the time of trouble.

Nothing could be more normal at certain times than to feel discouraged. But nothing could be more destructive than to allow that discouragement to breed self-pity.

One thing that helps us not to let that happen is to realize the purpose for discouragement.

Discouragement's Valuable Purpose

Discouragement warns us that something is wrong, and in that sense, serves a valuable purpose. Says Steve Harris, "I like to think of discouragement as Philip Yancey describes pain: it's useful in that it tells us something is not right, something is out of order. I shouldn't be happy about apathy and lethargy in a congregation. If that didn't discourage me, I wouldn't be normal." So feeling discouraged is normal in a world where very many things are "out of order." Maybe our body has been overtaxed; the discouragement signals us to slow down, to get some rest. Or perhaps we're in conflict with a troublesome family in the church; discouragement causes us to withdraw, to pull away until we can gain strength and perspective.

That view of discouragement doesn't come naturally to us. The experience hits us too painfully, and we feel bad about it, as though we'd done something wrong to feel this way. But there is benefit in identifying the cause, for then we are able to work on it. Eugene Peterson says, "I try to identify the sense of discouragement. At times, mine has been really symptomatic of a vocational hunger for something better, deeper, more authentic. If my discernment is right, if my interpretation is right, then that sense of discouragement is really a hopeful thing, because it shows that there's something alive there that longs for something different." In Eugene's case, the discouragement that led him to the Session to say "I quit," some seventeen years ago, also led him to discover he wasn't doing the job he felt called to be doing. He and the Session made adjustments, and today he is able to focus more of his energies on the pastoral tasks of prayer and study, which he loves. Discouragement, oddly, became the impetus for something better and more fulfilling.

Discouragement also drove a Midwest pastor we'll call Larry toward a higher goal. When Larry came to his church nine years ago, he braced himself. "The congregation had gone through squabbles and painful splits," he says, "and I didn't think healing would come for a long, long time.

"But God worked faster than I thought possible. In about five years we saw the attendance return, the facility fill up. We went to two worship services and two Sunday schools, and we completely redecorated and refurbished the sanctuary." Though some of the early years were difficult, it seemed that every dream of Larry's was coming true.

But then discouragement set in.

"I never had what you would call a midlife crisis in my

forties," Larry recalls, "because there was always so much that needed to be done and that I wanted to do. In a way I was too busy to have one. But then all of a sudden, there was no major challenge in front of me. I'd done everything I'd wanted to do, and I couldn't see anything else worth working toward. All I had left was going into a maintenance mode, and the thought of that killed me.

"I sank into the most difficult period of my life psychologically. I felt aimless, stuck. I was ready to leave; if somebody would have offered me a good-paying job selling garages, I probably would have taken it.

"As I was groping around for a new challenge, I realized our own county was going to experience good growth over the next decade. If the church was willing to 'lengthen the cords and strengthen the stakes' and really accept the challenge for growth — even if that meant relocation — there'd be plenty of exciting things ahead.

"But as I put out feelers in the church, all the readings were for keeping the status quo, complacency. People were beefing about the irritation of having to hold back-to-back services and two Sunday schools; they would never stand still for something larger than that. I thought, *How can any church that claims to be a New Testament church settle down to maintain its ministry when all around it are people who need to be reached?* I got angry about that. I internalized it, and soon it turned into depression, as it usually does."

This second wave of discouragement proved too much for Larry. He spent a good portion of that year looking for an opportunity to leave. Most of the positions he made contact with, though, didn't hold out any challenge for him. "I would simply have been leaving a maintenance ministry to go to a maintenance ministry," he says. "What was the sense in that?"

Then Larry received correspondence from a large church in a nearby state. The position looked exciting. As the interview process progressed smoothly, Larry's heart began to lift. The call committee narrowed the choices to Larry and one other. It looked likely that he would get the call, and then a frontier would open before him.

But the committee went with the other candidate.

"I felt trapped," he says. "I was in such a dilemma. I didn't want to leave just to be leaving. But I knew God had called and gifted me to do more than keep people happy and maintain things. And now the one option that looked promising fell through. I felt more discouraged than ever."

It was then that Larry, intuitively perhaps, began to channel that overwhelming sense of frustration toward something he wanted most of all. "I couldn't see clearly for a long while what my discouragement was coming from. But as I pinpointed it to my need for a new challenge, I thought, *What could be a bigger challenge than trying to lead* this *congregation into the growth I can see for it?* I knew these people, and by now I'd built a level of trust with them. If anybody was going to do it, it would be me.

"But at the same time, I didn't see how I possibly could convince them to try something so radical — to buy land, build a new facility, relocate. A consultant told me I was crazy for thinking a church in this staid community would ever go for something like that. Somehow, though, that in itself spurred me on. I began to dream again."

When I talked with Larry not long ago, he showed me a brand-new long-range plan for the church. "I envision a developing campus," he said excitedly. "We have the potential to develop the finest preschool in our state. On Sunday night we had our first congregational meeting to present the plan, and the first sampling showed 75 percent support. We've got a long way to go yet; nothing's for sure at this point. But I couldn't imagine being anywhere else. This is what God had for me."

As Larry learned, a pastor's discouragement, when its source is accurately determined, can drive him or her to something better. It can serve a good and useful purpose.

1. D. Martyn Lloyd-Jones, *Spiritual Depression: Its Causes and Cure* (Grand Rapids, Mich.: Eerdmans, 1973).
2. Archibald D. Hart, *Coping with Depression in the Ministry and Other Helping Professions* (Waco, Tex.: Word, 1984), 18.
3. Bartholomew Gottemoller, *Why Good People Suffer* (New York: Vantage Press, 1987), 2 – 4.
4. Oswald Chambers, *My Utmost for His Highest* (New York: Dodd, Mead & Company, 1935), 287.
5. C. S. Lewis, *The Screwtape Letters* in *The Best of C. S. Lewis* (Grand Rapids, Mich.: Baker Book House), preface.
6. Elisabeth Elliot, *Shadow of the Almighty* (San Francisco: Harper & Row, 1979).
7. Hart, 11.
8. Chambers, 137.

ELEVEN

CAN I LET ON THAT I'M DOWN?

Alone I cannot serve the Lord effectively, and he will spare no pains to teach me this. He will bring things to an end, allowing doors to close and leaving me ineffectively knocking my head against a wall until I realize that I need the help of the Body as well as of the Lord.

WATCHMAN NEE

When I got to my first church, because I was so green, they asked a godly and experienced elder who had moved away to come back and help me for a week," remembers Glen Parkinson. "One of the first things he told me as he oriented me to the church was this: 'Glen, you are not to have any friends in the church. It's not allowed; you just can't do that. No personal friends. That leads to cliquishness, and you'll antagonize some folks.

" 'Now we want you to be personable, to love everybody, but you can't talk about anything of a personal nature in this church. Find pastors or somebody outside this church, but don't do that kind of talking here.'

"Not all congregations feel that way," Glen continues, "but most ministers I know don't feel they're allowed to talk about problems in the church with anyone. If they do, people think they're being overly critical or they're gossiping. And pastors simply are not allowed to talk about personal problems. They're not allowed to have them.

"That's going to destroy any human being. It's no surprise it should happen to a pastor."

Laments Gary Downing, executive minister of Colonial

Church in Edina, Minnesota: "Feeling isolated, alone, that nobody understands or cares — it's a disease that seems to strike leaders. I bristle at the idea that leaders have to be lonely. Yet I look around and the landscape is littered with lonely leaders."

Why You Can't Talk

The reason so many leaders are lonely? Several powerful factors keep them from sharing personal concerns with people in the church.

People can't accept the pastor being down. One Southern Baptist pastor has tried at various times to share his discouragement with individuals in his congregation. The result? "I've opened up and had the door really slammed in my face. People have said, 'Well, you really shouldn't be discouraged. After all, you are a minister! You should pray about it.' They couldn't accept the fact that I was discouraged.

"Some have responded in a supportive way, but I've found it's a gamble talking to church members about your periods of discouragement. They still, many of them, have a feeling that a minister should not become discouraged."

Another consideration: *Much can't be shared without hurting the people involved.* "With some things, I have the feeling there's nobody I can talk to," admits a United Church of Christ minister, "because it deals with people they see every Sunday sitting in the pews."

"*Pastoral discontent can be contagious, injecting a negative mentality,*" is another reason, suggested by Gene Getz, pastor of Fellowship Bible Church North in Plano, Texas. To admit that you're down about Sunday's low attendance or a slump in giving may cause others to get down, too, and that would only exacerbate the problem. One pastor who's felt the tension is Harley Schmitt, of Brooklyn Park (Minnesota) Lutheran Church: "I'm keenly aware that the members of this congregation will not rise above their leadership. That's true everywhere. So it's immensely important for me as a pastor to provide positive leadership." And that precludes the sharing of some feelings of discouragement.

Perhaps the biggest reason pastors hesitate to talk about their discouragement with parishioners is they fear, wisely, *their despondency may push a hurting person further down*. And yet their responsibility as spiritual leaders is to strengthen — to never break off a bruised reed, however inadvertently. Teresa of Avila knew the concern when she wrote to fellow members of her religious order, "Let no one be . . . turned away from the life of virtue and religion by your gloom and morosity."

Eugene Peterson discovered this through a painful experience. "When my daughter, Karen, was in her teen years, she was giving my wife and me so much trouble," he remembers. "It was awful. One morning I walked into the church office and said to three or four women who were working there, 'I quit. I'm not going to be a parent anymore. I've had it.' I said it kind of tongue-in-cheek, but I was feeling that way, too.

"A couple of weeks later one of those women said to me, 'Don't ever do that again, because I've been having problems, and when you came in and said that, I thought, *If you can't handle it, how am I ever going to handle it?*'

"She was right," Eugene reflects. "As much as I don't believe in keeping a stiff upper lip, any congregation has a lot of people who are just barely making it at times. They've got guilt, and burdens, and sorrow, and discouragement — it's incredible what they're living with. So for me to be careless and throw in something like that was a stupid thing to do, I think. I was her pastor and a source of stability for her. And at that moment I was so full of my own frustration, I didn't care about hers."

Why You CAN Talk

Despite the risks and the legitimate reasons not to share their discouragement with their congregations, many pastors have taken a deep breath and done it. And they've found that in the appropriate setting it can be a refreshing and healthy experience — both for them and their people.

Here's why.

First, when a pastor reveals his or her pain, *it lets lay people know they're normal when they get down*. In a sense, such sharing becomes a ministry to the hurting by helping them realize suffering is the province of everyone, no matter how righteous. Says Frank Mercadante, "If I don't share my sins and weaknesses, I mislead the congregation. I make it look like I don't have clay feet, and then when they start seeing their own clay feet, they think there's something wrong with them. *The pastor has never met any problems*, they think. So I need to make a practice of making myself vulnerable."

A second reason pastors share is reflected in an old rabbinic story told by Madeleine L'Engle, the Newberry Award–winning writer. A student comes to his rabbi and says, "Oh, Rabbi, I love you!"

"Do you know what hurts me?" the rabbi asks him.

"Rabbi, I just told you that I love you. Why then do you ask me this irrelevant question?"

"Because if you do not know what hurts me," the rabbi answers, "how can you say you love me?"[1]

To love, people must first know where someone hurts. And *for a congregation to love its pastor, it must know where he or she hurts*. By sharing their discouragements with their people, many pastors have found themselves loved in a deeper way. "I thought I had to pretend," says a Midwest minister, "but the more I told people how I really felt, the more I got ministered to when I needed it. It sure beat harboring the hurt."

"I believe it can be a healthy thing for a church to learn their pastor is discouraged," adds Dave Dorpat, pastor of Faith Lutheran Church in Geneva, Illinois. "They see they have to do something, and they can come rally around him and start praying and ministering and assisting."

Contrary to the expected, *telling parishioners you're discouraged can actually help you stay*. Ed Bratcher explains why. "It's good to check out your feelings with somebody in the congregation whom you can trust. Ed White, an executive with the

Presbyterian churches in the Capital area, thinks most pastors move too quickly because they are discouraged and feel they have not been able to accomplish what they should have. And if only they would check it out with someone, they would find they have accomplished more than they think.

"So I'm learning to go to people and say, 'Give me a reading on this. This is what I see. I feel discouraged because of this. Is this how you see the situation?' They usually give me a fresh, more positive perspective."

Whom Can You Trust?

When you've admitted your discouragement and been blasted, and then risked it again and been blessed, you quickly sort the reasons.

The key difference, usually, is the person to whom you confess that you're down. The trick is finding those blessed people within the congregation with whom you can talk freely.

That's not partiality; that's practicality. John tells us that "Jesus did not trust himself" to the people in Jerusalem during the Passover festival "because he himself knew what was in their hearts" (John 2:24–25). But he did reveal himself openly to his trusted Twelve, and within that group, even more closely to Peter, James, and John. Jesus knew people's hearts and decided whether to trust himself to them accordingly.

Here are characteristics worth looking for in confidants, according to pastors who have sometimes learned the hard way.

One person to avoid discussing your discouragement with is a member who, in his or her favor, usually is heavily involved in the church, works hard, and enjoys hanging around the church office. This person shows interest in your family and ministry, at least measured by the questions he or she asks. But gradually you discover that something you told him or her got out to people you'd never intended to have hear it. You've found the parish gossip. Every church has at least one, and may the Lord have mercy on pastors in new churches until they find out who they are. "You don't make yourself vulnerable to the parish gossip," says one pastor. "You just don't."

Another check for prospective confidants: When they hear about problems from someone, do they quickly verbalize things such as "Oh, don't worry," or "Don't be afraid"? As one Lutheran pastor put it, "To a discouraged person, those are ridiculous things to be saying." What you want instead, says this pastor, who has developed close friends within his church, "is someone who will listen and then be willing to say in various ways, 'I'll stick with you; let's walk together; let's get together and pray.'"

A quality to accompany this: Can they lovingly confront people? As one pastor wrote on the LEADERSHIP survey, "One resource a pastor has for staying power is a friend(s) who understands and will confront."

Sympathy, a precious gift, ultimately falls short when it's not coupled with loving confrontation. The person to whom we risk personal things must know how to correct us when we need it. Deep down that's what we long for. Sympathy alone won't keep a ministry going. As Oswald Chambers knew, "The people who do us good are never those who sympathize with us; they always hinder, because sympathy enervates. No one understands a saint but the saint who is nearest to the Saviour."[2]

Steve Harris found such a person while candidating for his first church in Worcester, Massachusetts. "I was all gung-ho right out of seminary," he remembers. "I had all these ideals. I came in to the interview with the search committee and I laid out all these dreams and plans, and some of the people were really eating it up. But there was one guy, Larry, who was head of all the prisons in Massachusetts at the time. He was originally from down South, and he said in this real quiet voice, 'Steve, I've been sitting here for an hour listening to what you're going to do for us. How are you going to let us take care of you?' My first reaction was to think, *Oh, I'm not going to need that. I'm just, you know,* . . . but then I stopped. It was a beautiful question."

Additional traits have been pointed out by H. B. London, pastor of the First Church of the Nazarene in Pasadena, California, who has met with a particular church member for prayer each week for years. "I looked for someone who was not going to dump on me all the time," he says. "I looked for a person who has been wounded somewhere along the way. And I looked for someone who would not sit there in shock if I shared something heavy.

"When I was in Salem, Oregon," he says, "my prayer partner was a backhoe operator. He'd come into my office with muddy boots, and we'd sit and pray together for a half hour or so, then he'd get up and go on his way. We got to know each other and could share openly, and I took him on the mission field with me a couple of times. He caught the fever. He and his family sold their house and became full-time missionaries in South America.

"Here in Pasadena I meet weekly with a fifth-grade school teacher. He comes in after school one afternoon a week and we talk for a while, and pray, and read Scripture. With both of these men, I've shared crisis times in the family or in my own ministry. I could do it without any hesitancy because I knew what I shared wouldn't go any further."

The search for those supportive members is worth the time and trouble, for when you're discouraged, they will often be the ones to keep you going. "The single most helpful ingredient in keeping me going during the first four years here was the relationship I had with one man in the church," says John Yates. "Charlie and his wife came into the church the same time we came, and we began meeting for breakfast every Wednesday morning.

"I also had a small group of men I was trying to disciple, and we met every week to study the Scripture together. But Charlie was a peer. In no sense did I feel I was trying to lead him or teach him. He was right at my level. And he was as committed to seeing this church turned around as I was. He shared my vision completely.

"So whenever we would meet, he would ask me questions: 'How's this going? How's that going?' And if I'd be down, he'd really encourage me. He was a Barnabas to me. There were weeks when I lived for that breakfast. My wife and I have the same relationship, but sometimes you need more than your wife to give you that little upbuilding. And Charlie encouraged me and encouraged me and encouraged me.

"Then after four years, he felt God calling them to the mission field in Europe and he left. It broke my heart. I didn't think I was going to be able to make it without him. I had come to depend on him in a way that I had never depended on another man. It wasn't an unhealthy thing; it was a wonderful thing.

"But when he left, God brought another man along who filled the same role in my life. And Charlie has come back from Europe. He's been through kind of a difficult time. We're meeting again, but now I'm more in the role of encourager to him."

What Can You Say to "the Many"?

By definition, the number of these "best friends" a pastor can have in a congregation is small. Usually it's only a handful with whom you develop an "I can share almost anything" relationship.

But meanwhile, you're pastor of the whole flock. You've got to relate honestly and directly with everyone, even if you don't talk on the most personal level. What can you say —and not say — about your discouragement to the many members of your congregation you meet each week? When they ask you, "How are you doing?" what are your options?

"I think it's important to differentiate between the sharing of information and the sharing of feelings," says Gary Downing. "Sharing information can be damaging and can break a confidence because I'm talking about somebody else. I learned from the Navy that when it comes to information, you have to remember the phrase 'the need to know.' Who needs to know this?

"But sharing how I'm feeling right now is simple self-disclosure. I've learned I can tell people how I'm feeling without going into all the reasons for feeling that way.

"It started with my secretary; I began to give her fair warning when I was grumpy or out of sorts. I'd say, 'It doesn't have anything to do with you, but I'm feeling crummy today. Watch out for me.' I was able to be honest and relate to her person to person without disclosing personal details."

Robert Norris at Bethesda, Maryland's, Fourth Presbyterian Church followed the principle recently. "We'd been having some hard times, and one lady came in to the office and said, 'The Lord awakened me at four o'clock this morning to pray for you. Are you all right?'

" 'No, I'm not,' I said. 'I can't share all the reasons behind that, but thank you for your prayers. I'm deeply grateful for them.'

"And that was enough for her. She understood that and accepted it."

But when you're discouraged and most likely to say something hurtful, you're also least likely to monitor what you're saying. It calls for constant vigilance. A Midwest pastor admitted, "On Sunday nights, after the evening service, I'm wiped out. The adrenalin drops, and my defenses come down. I used to invite people over after services on Sunday nights, but I've found that's a dangerous thing to do. It was too easy for me then, especially when I was discouraged, to start ripping into things or criticizing people." When you're deeply discouraged and out of control, then it's probably not time to gather around you "the many." That's the time to call "the few," the chosen ones who can handle your rantings and ravings — and keep on loving you.

What Can You Say from the Pulpit?

On Sunday, though, no matter how discouraged you may feel, you've got to mount the steps to the pulpit. What a tension. On the one hand, you want to bring a refreshing, faith-inspiring word to hurting people. On the other hand, you're hurting yourself. You can't hypocritically hide that, but you don't want to add your burdens to others'. How can you express your honest discouragement without simply dumping on people? And how can you be helpful without putting up an "everything is fine" facade?

Pastors take radically different approaches, depending on a number of factors.

"I don't share my emotional tiredness or spiritual fatigue with my congregation," says a pastor of a small church in the mid-Atlantic states. "I have never felt good about dumping my emotional stuff on them."

Another pastor, of a large church, concurs: "It may be the right thing to do, but I have never felt free to say, 'Friends, I'm discouraged.' I always concern myself with that number among the two thousand on a Sunday morning for whom that would be too difficult to cope with — that the pastor feels that way. I'm the only one who would reap any benefit from that."

But some ministers have been forced through difficult circumstances to share their genuine, present-tense discouragement with a congregation, at least at times. Steve Harris is one.

"My son Matthew was born with spina bifida, and for the first year he was alive, he was in intensive care," Steve says. "We were essentially living there. Every day I'd see my son suffering, and kids on the floor were dying almost daily. Talk about a war zone! An intensive care unit for kids is a bitter place. It was virtually impossible to live there and not bring that discouragement and pain into my preaching. But I'd heard that pastors, young pastors especially, are supposed to preach their convictions and not their doubts. So I didn't share anything personal about what I was going through or how I was feeling.

"Every Sunday I'd come from a week of medical crises, and stress and tension at home. I'd hold it in. After awhile, I found myself pulling away from the people. I preached a whole sermon one time and didn't mention God's name, because I didn't want to deal with any of that stuff personally, publicly.

"I kept thinking, *The church shouldn't have to deal with a discouraged pastor. After all, I'm supposed to be the example of faith here; I'm supposed to be lifting them up. I can't be talking about how angry I am with God or how hard it is not to have prayers answered.*

"Then one night Matthew's stomach actually exploded. He was rushed into surgery, and it wasn't all over until about 1:30 in the morning. To go from that into the pulpit finally became more than I could take. One Sunday morning I broke down in the middle of my sermon and began crying.

"From that, I learned I needed to keep more current accounts with my emotions and find ways to tell people —not in a way that would hurt them but in a way that was authentic. If a pastor is going to be authentic, if his ministry is going to be effective, he's got to share those doubts in the appropriate ways. And as I began to take chances, to do that, I saw that God would use that, and it wasn't detrimental."

Sharing personal discouragement from the pulpit will never be easy. But it helps, when that's necessary, to realize that such self-disclosure can benefit the congregation. In *Where Is God When It Hurts?* Philip Yancey tells of a Midwest pastor who "was reading Psalm 145 from the pulpit. He tried to concentrate, but something was plaguing him: his week-old grandson had just died, grieving the whole family. He couldn't continue reading the words about God's goodness and fairness. His voice choked, he stopped reading, and he told the tense congregation what had happened.

" 'As people left the church,' he remembers, 'they said two important and helpful things:

" '1. "Thank you for sharing your pain with us."

" '2. "I grieve with you." This simple statement was the most helpful thing said. I did not feel alone. . . . They embraced my grief.' "[3]

From experiences such as these, pastors who conscientiously avoid mentioning their discouragement from the pulpit, as well as pastors who think it's worth the risk, have come to some common ground. On a Sunday when they're down, they return to principles such as these.

Sermons inevitably are shaped by our personal experience. Though we may not mention our discouragement directly, the sermon's tone and direction will probably reflect it, even if unconsciously. But that can help us preach more empathetically to parishioners who are on the ropes. "Many times my wife will come home from the service and say, 'Boy, you really preached to yourself today, didn't you?' " says H. B. London. "And I probably did. The sermon was probably born out of struggles that I was having. But that's okay. Because if I'm having them, lots of folks may be having them."

John Yates recently preached a sermon on discouragement, and "it prompted more response in this church than any I've preached in a long time. I think the reason was it grew out of some personal experience. I was discouraged about some marriages in the congregation that were going downhill, yet the people involved were not facing up to their problems. And a friend, a leader in ministry, had gone through a difficult experience and was not facing up to his own mistakes in ministry. I was so upset about those things that I preached with a little more passion than usual. Evidently it really struck home."

To whatever extent you share your discouragement, do it in the context of God's faithfulness. Says Yates: "If I share with the congregation, 'I've had a discouraging time this week,' I try to always do it in the context of 'But God is good. God is faithful.' " Harley Schmitt amplifies the principle: "You can communicate to your people that you're hurting, but you can communicate in such a way that they know you're still trusting in the Lord and that you're waiting on the Lord and that God is faithful. Then that gives them a sense of encouragement, too."

Among other things, that may mean riding out the time of discouragement until you can say that honestly. Says a Presbyterian minister: "I find it better to tell people of the discouragements I have been through rather than ones I am currently engaged in. Once I've been through them, they become natural illustrations from my past."

Recently I read of a survey in which members of a church answered this question: "Why do you attend here?" The answers people gave: (1) Our pastor is one of us; (2) He gives us hope.

In these survey results lies the key to preaching when we're discouraged. We can in various ways share our discouragement with the people, so they know we're one of them. But always, and in every way, we point to God's faithfulness; we give hope.

Fellow Leaders

Because of the various constraints on talking to people within the congregation, some pastors find they can open up best to key leaders — other staff members or carefully chosen lay leaders who understand the church and the ministry but can give some perspective. "After ten years in ministry, my greatest sense of encouragement has been this year," wrote a pastor on the LEADERSHIP survey, "because I'm finally on staff in a team situation. It's great to be committed to each other and sense support, and therefore be able to reach higher goals. The other pastor has become a close friend with whom I can share openly and honestly; we can laugh together."

When a staff situation is good, as the old nursery rhyme puts it, "it's very, very good."

But likewise, "when it is bad, it's horrid."

"The loneliest feeling you'll ever have in ministry can be in a staff situation," says an East Coast pastor who has been in both good and bad ones. "After coming to one church, I asked the senior pastor what I should call him, if I should use his first name. He said, 'Well, we'll see.' It was clear he didn't want me to do that."

A safe professional distance easily widens into a professional Grand Canyon that's nearly impossible to cross. The gulf comes from the natural hesitancy to let colleagues see you hurting and in need of help.

To get over that, it often helps to begin small, to share the daily discouragements first. Gary Downing tells this story: "This morning a young staff member working in youth ministry here came in and said, 'How are you doin'?' I so easily could have said, 'Fine, things are going fine,' and he would have gone on his way. But instead I stopped and said, 'John, I'm down. I am sick of process, of going through all these motions to get anything done. I was at a search committee meeting last night till eleven o'clock dealing with questions for an interview with a prospective youth worker. We finally came to a conclusion and wrote some questions that reflected the values of the group, but it took us three and a half hours to get there. Then this morning I was up early for a breakfast meeting about the men's group, and it was the same old story: it took forever to make a decision because we had to allow everyone to speak his mind. I'm sick and tired of how time consuming all that is.'

"And John looked at me and said, 'Yeah, that's the congregational way, isn't it? We kind of lift our cups to that: Skol to the congregational way.'

"Boy, that helped. I didn't need therapy for my discouragement; I didn't need any advice. I just needed to acknowledge it and shake my fist about it. John listened, gave me a pat on the back, and walked away, and I felt about five pounds lighter."

From that kind of experience, we learn to trust fellow staff members with our moments of deeper darkness. Carolyn Weese, for many years a staff associate at Hollywood (California) Presbyterian Church, writes of a staff retreat she helped arrange: "When the day came and I began the drive to the retreat, I began to wonder why I was even going. What did I have to offer? I surely expected nothing from it.

"Following dinner, we gathered for a time of Bible study and caring and praying for one another. As I listened to my brothers and sisters share their needs, I suddenly, for the first time, was face to face with the fact I was spent, used up, burned out. Sitting there quietly, my first thought was to run. How could I ever tell them what had been happening to me? What would happen if I shared my pain with them? Whatever would they say if they knew I was the weak link in the chain? No, I couldn't, and wouldn't, say a word."

But Carolyn finally decided to say something, and when she did, "three members of the staff whom I love dearly, and who have had very strategic roles in my life, gathered around me and prayed for me. Through their prayers . . . I could actually feel a healing process begin to take place.

"On Sunday, I came to church and did all the usual things that are expected of me on a Sunday, but I also worshiped."[4]

The risk of confessing our discouragement to fellow leaders may be great, but as most have found, the rewards are greater.

An Outside Chance

For many ministers, though, the best chance of finding a person with whom they can share their deepest discouragements comes outside the church.

"I've never had the expectation that the congregation would be my spiritual support," says one minister. "I know some ministers feel they should, but I've always made sure I got it someplace else. I have friends and a spiritual director outside."

There are some good reasons for going outside to find confidants. For one thing, ministers move frequently, and for at least a few years in a new church you'll probably still be closer to friends from previous years — from seminary or earlier churches.

But the biggest reason stems from the nature of an intimate friendship. Explains Gary Downing, "Only with a special kind of friend can you talk about the four issues we all struggle with: money, sex, power, and time. We're always facing opportunities but also dangers with these. Most Christian leaders I've encountered have no one, including their spouse, with whom they can talk candidly about struggles with money, sex, power, or time."

These sensitive issues are the kind that generally are not appropriate to discuss with members of a congregation, because they either deal with others in the church or cause unnecessary ripples of confusion or fear. And that means the building of a friendship with someone outside.

"It's great having someone outside, away from the situation, who honestly wants to know, 'How's it going?' " says one pastor. "But building that kind of friendship is tough because church life tends to eat up your time. You don't have a lot of hours left over. So you have to make it happen."

How did Gary handle the time problem? "About nine years ago, while I was working with Young Life, I met a guy named Rob, a young, rising business executive from the right side of the tracks. I grew up on the wrong side of the tracks. He was single; I was married. We didn't have a lot in common, but as he began to drop by once in a while, I discovered his concept for his life was similar, focused on friendship with God and being himself with other people. We started jogging together and playing racketball together. I began to look at him as a close friend, and after a while I started relying on him as a sounding board for things.

"We really enjoyed getting together, but our schedules were so crazy that we could go for weeks and never talk. Then one fall afternoon we went for a walk around a local lake and decided we would try something together: once a week for a year we would get together just to talk, and we would talk about 'our highest ideals and our deepest needs.' But we would never share more than we felt comfortable talking about. At the time it seemed funny that we had to be so intentional about developing a better friendship, but we both saw that with the pace of ministry life in America, if it wasn't on the calendar, it wouldn't happen.

"As we got together and the weeks went by, we had a lot of fun. We found we could talk about those four tough areas, and just talking about them somehow made them more manageable. Power needs, struggles with money, sexual fantasies — they weren't hard to share when you knew you weren't going to get advice or lectures but just a listening ear from a friend who was committed to you.

"We're in our ninth year together. I view Rob as my closest friend, second only to my wife, closer than a brother. I can't think of anything I sooner or later wouldn't be able to tell Rob except for the most intimate aspects of my marital relationship. I get tearful talking about it because it's so important to me. I think for me that friendship has been a key in keeping me alive and growing through tough years of ministry."

Care Network

Each one of the above resources, inside or outside the congregation, can be a place to turn when you're discouraged, a place where you can let on that you're down.

But two are better than one. And three are better than two. When your emotions are being divebombed, you need all hands on deck. You need many people who will listen, who will pray, who will stick by you. Writes Jim Stobaugh, pastor of Fourth Presbyterian Church in Pittsburgh: "My network of care — spouse, spiritual director, support group, and times of solitude — were present when my congregation nearly fired me. They were present when I needed to be told I was too hard on a congregant. They were there when I needed to hear that I was ignoring my wife. They were present when my father suddenly died of cancer. They encouraged me to continue pursuing a program when I was ready to scrap it. They enabled me to stand firm in the face of temptation and adversity."

The whole network of care — without that, many pastors would not be in the ministry today.

---

1. Madeleine L'Engle, "The Door Interview," *The Wittenburg Door* (December 1986 – January 1987).

2. Oswald Chambers, *My Utmost for His Highest* (New York: Dodd, Mead & Company, 1935), 223.

3. Philip Yancey, *Where Is God When It Hurts?* (Grand Rapids, Mich.: Zondervan, 1977), 150.

4. Carolyn Weese, "From the Fire Back into the Frying Pan," (1987, unpublished).

T W E L V E

THE DECISION TO STAY

It's always too soon to quit.

V. RAYMOND EDMAN

Is it time to leave my church? Maybe even the ministry?

Those questions, though seldom spoken, are often thought. The LEADERSHIP survey showed nearly 40 percent of pastors have "considered leaving" the pastorate and "looked into other types of ministries and/or occupations." That doesn't include the nearly 10 percent who did indeed give it up. And the number who have wrestled with "Should I leave this current church?" probably approaches 100 percent.

The question is one of the most difficult a pastor will have to answer, for it is almost always, as one put it, "filled with lingering doubts, self-criticisms, and the pain of unfulfilled dreams."

Though the question "Should I leave?" occasionally plays in every pastor's mind, within the discouraged minister it puts on a full-court press. It dogs, it harries, it doesn't let up. "There have been many times when I've questioned, 'Lord, what are you saying?' " says a Lutheran pastor. " 'Does this mean my ministry is finished here? Or finished period? Are you calling me into something else?' And sometimes in a fit of frustration I cry out, 'Lord, I'm finished; I'm done!' "

Exit or Endure?

The question ultimately offers two options: stay or leave. There's no middle ground. You can't "halfway" leave.

Yet often emotions stay in the middle zone, attracted first to leaving, then to staying, then back to leaving. Each option holds pros and cons, and neither is easy.

At that moment you long for a direct, strong assurance from God that his will is one option or the other. But when you're discouraged, that's not easy to determine. Turning to Scripture for guidance may not clear your mind. On the one hand, Jesus "set his face like flint" to go up to Jerusalem. *He didn't turn away from difficulty; neither should I.* But at other times Jesus left Judea and Galilee; he changed ministry sites to the other side of the Jordan to avoid further confrontation with the Jewish authorities. Stay or leave? Each is right — at the right time. But how do you determine what time it is?

Our ultimate goal, of course, is continued faithfulness to God and service of him. But given our current situation, could that be in a different church or even in a setting outside the pastoral ministry? Something has to give — but is that something an attitude within as God teaches us to endure? Or is that something the situation without as God shows us that "a bruised reed he will not break" and "he provides a way of escape"?

Pastors who have grappled with "Is it time to leave?" during their dark periods have learned they can't answer that question until they first ask themselves several others. Here are ones they pose to themselves.

Questions Worth Asking

Am I free to pursue the essentials of ministry? No setting is without its limitations, of course. Harold Myra, president of Christianity Today, Inc., reminds us of Joe Bayly's concept that "all of us find ourselves in a box. It may be a big box or a small one . . . but we all find ourselves in a box of limitations and opportunities. Our task is not to bemoan the limitations or strut because of the size of the box. If we've committed ourselves to the situation, we try to understand the box and fill it — every corner and cranny — with all the creativity and energy possible."[1]

But sometimes a ministry "box" may have the lids closed and taped shut; soon it becomes difficult even to breathe. A pastor in the East realized that even after several years in a congregation, "I didn't have any freedom to provide leadership. The board, though not where it should be in terms of spiritual maturity, had a tremendous amount of power and wasn't about to give it up. I couldn't see that changing in the future. My relationship was cordial with all of them, but in that situation, I couldn't lead the church." If our every move is blocked and it takes all our energy to survive, let alone minister, then it's probably time to go.

The reason *probably* is a key word is illustrated in the experience of one Southern pastor. "I came to this church to build a ministry of discipleship. Yet in my early years, every effort in that direction was stymied. Inner pain began to build, and I became desperate to get out. I even had several opportunities to move. But I never had an inner peace about leaving, so I stayed. Now, ten years later, my discipling is growing." The Lord often works through painful situations.

Overall, though, pastors have found help in candidly considering this question: "Given the inevitable resistance to change (and handful of cranky personalities) in any group, am I generally free to serve?"

Have I already left, internally? A friend of mine got swept up in a management war in his company some years ago. Even though he came out with only minor injuries, the months of rumors, firings, secret meetings, and reprisals made something snap within him. He suddenly realized one day, *I can't work for these people anymore.* He had lost his respect for them.

He continued to work for the company for a while after that, but inside, he had already left. That period proved the most difficult in his business career. "When you get to that point of leaving within," he realized, "there's no sense prolonging the inevitable. Find another place to go as soon as you can."

It's possible as well to leave a church while still preaching every Sunday. But that usually entails, as one pastor put it, "becoming mechanical, going through the motions." And it usually only makes us cynical or bitter within. For our own sake as well as the church's, it's better to leave. But if, despite the current difficulties, we still respect the congregation and hold a dream for our work with it, then staying is indicated.

Has my desire to leave been building for a long time, or is it a sudden response to recent events? "Today I feel as though I'd like to quit, take a leave of absence, resign from the world, or something!" wrote Don Bubna, pastor of Salem (Oregon) Alliance Church, in his journal several years ago. He'd been hit by a boxcar full of discouraging events. "We had just received another turndown from a potential youth pastor. The church seemed to be on a plateau, the elders stuck on dead center. . . . A young man from our congregation who had recently gone to Africa was killed in an automobile accident. A missionary pilot from our fellowship had been attacked by South Pacific islanders with machetes and almost died. A retired missionary, our esteemed pastor of visitation, passed into the presence of the Lord after a very brief illness.

"During this same period, I received four letters in one day marked PERSONAL. This kind of envelope seldom bears good news. One was a complaint from a long-time attender who felt I had gotten soft on the gospel. The person was leaving the congregation in order 'to be fed' elsewhere. Another was the resignation of a staff member with whom I had served for more than two decades."

When the discouragement comes like a horde of locusts, the natural feeling is to run. But Don stayed; he realized he'd had many great years with the church that the current events couldn't change. And there was a future beyond these events as well.

Immediate events don't tell the whole story, so "we need to not make a hasty decision," counsels Maynard Nelson, pastor of Calvary Lutheran Church near Minneapolis. "With all the clamoring around us, it takes time to quiet ourselves to hear the still, small voice of God."

Do my gifts and philosophy of ministry generally match my church's? A California pastor I know went to a small church and found his approach to ministry differed vastly from theirs. They wanted the standard format of midweek services and programs; he wanted to build the fellowship through a decentralized model of home groups. They wanted traditional music; he felt more contemporary music would aid outreach. "But I had been called to be their pastor," he said, "so I tried to be everything they wanted me to be." As a result, discouragement set in. When he went their way, he didn't feel happy; when he didn't, the congregation let him know it. That kind of incompatibility usually calls for a new start. In the words of one pastor who is involved in his denomination's placement work, "One of the big secrets of staying power is getting the right person in the right place. Conflict and discouragement inevitably come with a mismatch."

But in this California pastor's case, he decided to stay despite his discouragement. Over time he was able to communicate his vision for ministry to the board, and now, seven years later, they have embraced it wholeheartedly. The pastor and congregation now work together well.

Recognizing the studies that show it often takes seven to ten years for a pastor and congregation to fully mesh, it's also true, as one consultant writes, that "if the friction constantly produces sparks or if adaptation demands a major part of your energy, it may be an indication change is needed."

What is my normal inclination in tough situations? Andre Bustanoby describes his experience leading a church in California in the early seventies: "I was battered with discouragement because it seemed that *nothing* I did would stop the guerrilla warfare in the church. About 10 percent of the congregation was determined to get me out. I had 90 percent of the congregation with me and I felt, *I ought to win the war. I have the troops to do it.* It did not even occur to me to resign. I never give up. That's just not part of me.

"But then one night we were in a congregational meeting

and charges were being thrown back and forth. I remember sitting there watching this when I sensed the Lord saying, 'Andy, get up in front of that congregation and resign.' The reason why I knew that was God's voice is because I never would think anything like that. That was too atypical of my personality. But inside I knew, *That's your problem, Andy: you don't know when to stop hassling people to win. You've got to win regardless. You've done it in your marriage; now you're doing it in the church. When are you going to quit doing this?*

"That day marked a great advance in my spiritual growth. I discovered the marvelous truth that when I gave in, I was not destroyed. I had always feared I could never emotionally survive a defeat or even a strategic withdrawal, so I fought tooth and nail. At the time my marriage was in trouble for the same reason — I had to win every confrontation. My wife had stopped talking to me. But God led me against the grain of my personality. I resigned and gradually developed the ability to retreat, to give in, to surrender.

"From that whole experience I learned a principle that has helped me make major decisions. I call it the 'Bustanoby Rule of Thumb.' That is, listen extra hard to the idea that goes against your natural inclination, because that may very well be the voice of the Spirit. If you are like I was, a fighter and a never-say-die person, really scrutinize those inner urges to fight on, because you can do that too well by yourself. On the other hand, if your tendency is to walk away quietly, to never make waves, the Rule says, 'Watch out for that inner voice that is urging you to pull up your stakes, pack your tent, and move on. God's voice may be saying something very different.' "

Do I have the physical and emotional strength to stay on? Says a pastor in his thirties about his decision to leave, "I had to gauge how much more I could take personally. I decided I could take some more but I probably wouldn't last until the church turned around." For the sake of his long-term health and service in the kingdom, he found a much different church and today is feeling strong.

On the other hand, if you feel well physically and emotionally, it's an indicator for staying.

How much can my family endure? One veteran pastor wrote on the LEADERSHIP survey, "Once, when the board was being bossy and difficult, I did resign, but only because my wife was suffering from the conflict. It proved to be a good and wise move." Spouses and children may need emotional relief from a discouraging ministry situation. But if they're holding their own, it's another sign to stay.

Answering these questions may still yield a split decision — some factors that indicate staying, others that say it's time to leave. But ultimately, as Robert Norris, pastor of Bethesda, Maryland's, Fourth Presbyterian Church, suggests, "You must rely on your own human spirit."

Two pastors, both of whom were discouraged and longing to leave, chose entirely different paths. Here they explain their decisions.

One Who Decided to Stay

Eugene Peterson has served more than twenty-five years as pastor of Christ Our King Presbyterian Church in Bel Air, Maryland, northeast of Baltimore. That remarkably long tenure, considering the national average is somewhere in the three- to five-year range, has not exempted him from the time of decision.

"I can think of three times since I've been here," he admits, "when I was ready to leave. I tried my best to get out of here. I thought I had done everything I knew how to do and people were unappreciative. They didn't know how good they had it, and so I was going to show them. Those times weren't for just a couple of weeks; they lasted for seven, eight, or nine months.

"But as I'd search out other options, either nothing would open up or nothing would appeal to me. And finally, still in a funk, I'd sort of give up and think, *Shoot, if I've gotta stay here, I'll just stay here.* And then I'd see changes. I found myself working with the same people, working on the same things, but suddenly it was different — deeper and better. I'd notice significant changes in my life in terms of my understanding of spirituality and pastoral work. I take no credit for it, because I tried my best to leave. I'm so glad that by the grace of God I didn't. If I had left precipitously, I don't think I would have gone into these new areas in my life.

"In those times, my wife wasn't sure that staying was the right thing, because I wasn't much fun to live with. But now I'm so glad I didn't move."

One Who Decided to Leave

Another pastor we'll call Eric was in his fifth year of ministry with a particular church when he hit bottom. "Pressures kept building in the church and in me," Eric says. "The board and I couldn't agree on anything. The only way to get anything done was to go around them, and that didn't go along with my philosophy of ministry. I was not doing the kind of work I thought I should be doing. And I didn't have anybody I could share with. No one in the congregation even knew I was having any problems.

"The aloneness was deadly. I tried to talk to my wife about problems in the church. She loved me, but she couldn't do anything. So when I would tell her what people had done to me, she'd get angry. One night she said, 'I want to scratch their eyes out!' That wasn't a godly thing to instill in her, so I just quit talking about things."

Eric's relationship with his wife became strained. "Kelly said I wasn't the same person anymore, that my personality was changing. It was probably true, but I didn't know what to do about it. Sexual temptations skyrocketed for me. They were tough feelings to fight. Finally I got a little counseling. I didn't want to get counseling; I kept thinking, *Hey, I give counseling.* But I knew an older man who had been a pastor and who had kind of been keeping an eye on me anyway. I invited him over and spilled out everything. He mostly listened, and then he made a few objective statements about what I could and could not do in the situation. 'You can't change every situation, Eric,' he told me. That freed me.

"I had gone into the church thinking, *It's not the kind of situation I enjoy, but I'll work with it and change it. I can change pretty much anything if I just have enough faith and enough elbow grease.* Now I had given them five years of my life, and things hadn't changed at all. I realized it was going to take years to turn the church around. And I wouldn't last that long.

"Then I saw a telephone commercial, 'Reach out and touch someone.' The commercial gave me the idea to call an old friend, a dear friend. We were atheists together, were converted together, and went to seminary together. He was the best man at my wedding. So I called him and said, 'I'm not going to survive here, Don. I don't know what I'm going to do.'

"He kidded me, 'Well, I'm planting this church down here; why don't you come down, and we could work together?' We both laughed about it, but I couldn't get the idea out of my mind. I started pursuing it, and things worked out.

"People in the church had no notion I was having problems. They were sorry to see me go; it was all very nice and nostalgic. But I came here to save my marriage and to see if I could save my ministry. I went from being the senior pastor of the largest church in the district to being an associate pastor in a mission church. Everybody thought it was a step down.

"But here I wasn't alone. Don and I built a team ministry where there was genuine respect. He left a year ago now, to plant another church, but we talked about everything. We would talk about sermons we were going to preach.

"I found I could have friends in the church. I have people I can talk to. In fact, just the other night I told the board I was getting discouraged about our long-range planning, and we talked it out.

"And the marriage is fantastic. The last years have been tremendously healing. We have become intimate with each other the way it should be. I can talk to Kelly about the church.

"I was kept in the ministry by coming here. There is no

question about that. One of the more mature decisions I ever made was to leave."

Leave the Pastorate Altogether?

It's one thing to leave a church. It's quite another to leave the pastorate altogether.

When all strategies and prayers seem to have failed and you stand on the precipice wondering whether to jump and leave it all behind, there's a terrifying loneliness. *Has anyone — ever — faced what I am facing? Do they know my pain? What did they do?*

Indeed others have been there — and have survived. Here, briefly, are the true stories of three pastors who stood on the edge and wondered, *Should I give up the ministry?* They made very different choices.

"I felt like I had been beaten up," *Allen* (not his real name) says of his closing days in a New England pastorate. "I used to wake up on Sunday morning and dread going to church. My favorite time of the week was Sunday night because Sunday morning was behind me for another week. I wanted to leave the pastorate — just get out.

"I started looking around and found a good opportunity working with a social-service organization. The position connected several interests and skills I had. At the same time, I was asked to consider a position with a small church in another state. I thought, *Why bother? I don't want to go through all this again.* But somehow — and it's hard to explain this — I felt like I was being swept by a wave back into the church. All my circumstances and feelings began to move that direction again. So I did take the church interview. They extended a call, and after more deliberation, I decided to accept it.

"I was ready to leave the pastorate, but now after more than a year here at the new church, I can say there has been such healing. I would never say, 'I've learned how to deal with discouragement; I can forget about that now.' It's an ongoing struggle. But I wake up Sunday morning and look forward to going to church. I learned through this that God is watching over our decisions more than we think."

Don, a minister in Tennessee, came to a new church and found that one elder in the congregation opposed everything he did. After Don had been there three or four months, a bald lie about him began to circulate in the church. Eventually Don was able to trace the source of the lie directly to the troublesome elder. When the other elders confronted him with the facts in an elders' meeting, he admitted he had spread the lie, and he resigned. But then they rallied around the liar: "You don't need to resign," they said. "Stay on."

Don thought, *Is this the kind of elders I have? I don't have to put up with this.* He resigned immediately.

A registered nurse, Don took a position as supervisor of a nearby nursing home. "But in three months I was unhappy," he says. "I came home one day and told my wife, 'I've just got to go back to preaching.' I realized that I really did enjoy the ministry and that my decision to leave had been a spur-of-the-moment response when I was disgusted. Well, I guess it had been building: my previous congregation had not given me a salary increase in years, and the conflict in the elders' meeting touched off all that."

A nearby church became open, and within a month Don was back in the pastorate. "It's a smaller church, but very productive in many ways. It's been a happy ministry here." Don is now in his thirteenth year with the church. "I haven't regretted coming back," he says. "And I really haven't thought of leaving again."

Roger Landis, the pastor whose descent into discouragement was told in chapter 1, came to the point of considering suicide. In his desperate pain he cried out, "Lord, I just can't hack it, physically, emotionally, or spiritually. Lord, get me out of this place."

"And yet I could never consider leaving the pastorate," he

says. "That summer I was approached about a position as a nursing home chaplain. 'No way!' I said."

Roger began meeting often with Dick Berger, his district superintendent, to try to get a handle on the situation at church. They called a meeting with the church elder and the church chairman. "Both the elder and church chairman were supportive of me," Roger says, "but they realized the conflict in the church had gotten totally out of hand. For the sake of both the church and me, they thought it would be good if I resigned." They decided to let Roger stay in the parsonage with full financial support for several months or until he found another position.

Both a board member and administrator from the nursing home approached Roger about the position as chaplain again. Roger was offered the position. "I had until the end of the year to make a decision, and I had gotten a number of inquiries from churches, but somehow I sensed God was in it. God had softened my heart, and my feelings about nursing home chaplaincy had completely changed."

The position didn't start for several months. "That gave me months of no responsibility, and after what I'd been through they were heaven-sent. The first month or so I hardly did more than sleep late and go picnicking with my wife — whatever we felt like doing. We went to a church where we didn't know anybody, and it was a joy to go anonymously, sit together, and worship. I didn't have to think about any responsibility, even praying in front of anybody. It was grand. Those months were very healing."

And his new position? "I still feel I'm in the ministry," he says. "I feel very much at home here; I've learned to love these people. I've never had a more appreciative and sensitive congregation in my life. We've seen two come to know the Lord. We've started some programs, and I look forward to work each day. But I look forward to going home at night, too.

"One of the greatest delights about this work is not having to meet with the board of deacons or trustees. I don't have to juggle one hundred 'bosses.' So through it all, I'm so thankful for the hand of God. He kept me from self-destruction, and through that deep depression he showed me his grace in such a wonderful way. He still has use for me; he has fulfilling service for me to render."

In his own way, each of these three pastors demonstrates remarkable staying power. As F. Scott Fitzgerald has said, "Vitality shows not only in the ability to persist but in the ability to start over."

None would have chosen the events that led him to the point of considering leaving the pastorate. Each was driven to the decision by a hungry pack of circumstances that threatened his well-being. But are there common lessons that can be learned from these pastors' diverse experiences?

God was still there. Reflecting on his experience, Roger Landis says, "God was there. I praise him for that. I can't fault the way God has dealt with me. I love Jeremiah 29:11, ' "For I know the plans I have for you," declares the Lord, "plans to prosper you and not to harm you, plans to give you hope and a future." ' Without a sense of hope for the future, life is grim. But God was with me even then."

Healing from the events that led to the decision takes time. For Allen, it has taken over a year. Roger, now a year and a half from his resignation, says, "I never questioned God's love and his wisdom through that. But I've questioned a lot my own abilities. I saw how weak I was. I feared circumstances were going to get to the point where I couldn't handle them. But I'm beginning to rebuild a fair self-image again now." As one pastor explained, "If we're worn out, it's usually come over a long period of time. If we're going to be renewed, it takes time for that also."

God could and did use it for their ultimate good. In a recent study of ministers who had left the pastorate and then returned, one researcher found that two-thirds felt they were more empathetic with people as a result of their time away.

Andre Bustanoby, today a successful psychotherapist, writes that as he began his practice following his leaving pastoral ministry, "it required that I listen, be empathetic, and care about the pain of others, something I lacked in the pastorate. As a pastor, I could be warm and empathetic with people who liked me and whom I liked, but it was a new experience to truly care about people I didn't know, some of whom were positively unlovely."[2]

"Now I can understand someone who's lost all hope in life and who's depressed to the point where he wants to end it all," says Roger Landis. "Before, in my arrogance I might have thought, *Hey, come on, straighten up.* But now I understand."

Through God's grace, many who have left the pastorate do not think of their leaving strictly as an end but also as a beginning. They gradually have come to focus less on the pain than on what resulted from it. They encountered God's grace in a new way. They found they could serve him effectively in another calling.

The Unmistakable Decision

The decision to leave a church or the ministry will never be painless. But pastors have drawn comfort from a simple, surprising truth that Corrie ten Boom captured in the words, "Never be afraid to trust an unknown future to a known God."

Writes Calvin Ratz, pastor of Abbotsford (British Columbia) Pentecostal Assembly: "Once I had two options to consider. For some time I couldn't make up my mind. My head said one thing; my heart said another. In talking with my parents, my mother commented, 'I don't know what you will do, Cal, but I know you will do the right thing.'

"At first I brushed it off as the confidence any mother would have in her son. But that wasn't what she meant. She went on to explain, 'If your motives are right, and you are prayerful in making the decision, God will not let you make a mistake.'

"She was right. If you honestly want to move in God's will, he won't let you foul up a decision that affects his church.

"That doesn't mean all will turn out glowingly. There may

be hard times ahead in the church to which we are sure God sent us. Our ministry may even be rejected there after a while. But we will not be outside the larger channel of God's purpose for our shaping and growth."

Our decisions, no matter how difficult, can never take us beyond the loving reach of God.

In *Thoughts in Solitude*, Thomas Merton captures that most assuring of thoughts in a prayer called "The Road Ahead." It might be the prayer of every pastor who agonizes over the question, "Is it time to leave?"

My Lord God, I have no idea where I am going, I do not see the road ahead of me, I cannot know for certain where it will end. Nor do I really know myself, and the fact that I think I am following your will does not mean that I am actually doing so. But I believe that the desire to please you does in fact please you. And I hope I have that desire in all that I am doing. I hope that I will never do anything apart from that desire. And I know that if I do this you will lead me by the right road, though I may know nothing about it. Therefore, I will trust you always, though I may seem to be lost and in the shadow of death. I will not fear, for you are ever with me, and you will never leave me to face my perils alone.[3]

---

1. Harold Myra, ed., *Leaders* (Carol Stream, Ill. and Waco, Tex.: Leadership/Word, 1987), 18.
2. Andre Bustanoby, *A Reason for Hope When You Have Failed* (San Bernardino, Cal.: Here's Life Publishers, 1986).
3. Thomas Merton, *Thoughts in Solitude* (New York: Farrar, Straus & Giroux, 1976).

THIRTEEN

HIDDEN RESOURCES

Everything that comes to us like an assault of fate — dread of the future, human disappointments, embroilments in our life, trials and afflictions — all this becomes for him who has faith an element which can no longer swamp and bury him, but mysteriously bears him up, as Noah was borne by the flood.

HELMUT THIELICKE

The preceding chapters have offered pastors' insights into staying power — how to build an enduring ministry, how to persevere when discouragement strikes. Many of the allies mentioned have been external — a listening friend, a vacation, a supportive board.

But perhaps the most important secrets of staying power are the ones you can't see — the internal, hidden resources.

Ultimately, the minister called by God must be sustained by him. There may be periods when the people and things we had counted on for support fail us, turn against us, waste away. As David cried out from the dank recesses of a cave, "Look to my right and see; no one is concerned for me. I have no refuge; no one cares for my life" (Ps. 142:4). But even at that moment we are not alone: "I cry to you, O Lord; I say, 'You are my refuge, my portion in the land of the living' " (v. 5).

There is always one who cares for us.

The ministers who have endured, who have continued through the years without becoming cynical or hardened, have drawn deeply from what I call "God's TLC" — his truth, his love, and his call.

They are the three great secrets of staying power.

God's Truth

Arthur Holmes, professor of philosophy at Wheaton (Illinois) College, has written a book entitled *All Truth Is God's Truth*. I like that phrase. Truth is one of God's commodities, whatever the field of study. Whenever we come to grips with what is true in a situation, we come closer to God.

Discouraged pastors told me some of the pernicious *untruths* they have battled. There were lines of thinking they couldn't seem to shake during dark days: "I'm no good as a pastor," "I don't have what it takes," "There's no future for me," "I missed God's will in coming to this church."

Kent Hughes, pastor of College Church in Wheaton, wrestled with this syllogism during a time a church he had planted was declining in attendance: "God has called me to do something he hasn't given me the gifts to accomplish. Therefore, God is not good. I had been called by God, and now I was the butt of a cruel joke."

That's why God's truth is essential for staying power. During a crisis, it restores to us the correct perspective — his. J. Francis Peak has said, "The major cause of discouragement is a temporary loss of perspective. Restore proper perspective, and you take new heart."

Here are some fundamental truths that have helped depleted pastors take new heart.

I can expect difficulty both in life and in ministry. At first, that doesn't sound like uplifting news. You'll never see it as the inside verse of a card from Hallmark. But in *The Road Less Traveled*, Scott Peck explains why it assists us when we're troubled: "Life is difficult. This is a great truth, one of the greatest truths. It is a great truth because once we truly see this truth, we transcend it. Once we truly know that life is difficult — once we truly understand and accept it — then life is no longer difficult. Because once it is accepted, the fact that life is difficult no longer matters."[1]

Pastor Eugene Peterson illustrates the principle. "I'm a runner, but I have arthritic knees, and if the weather is a certain way those knees really hurt," he says. "There's not a whole lot I can do about them, and my natural reflex is to avoid the pain, but that only makes it worse — I tighten my muscles, I lose my running rhythm.

"But I've found that when I lean into the pain, kind of accept it and enter into it, it becomes less. And then I can continue.

"I think the image works for me when I encounter spiritual and emotional pain. There's always that struggle at the beginning: Am I going to go on? But when I say, 'I'm going to accept this,' I don't know what happens, but the acceptance starts to change it."

In short, discouragement will come to every pastor. That's not something anyone wants to hear. But accepting that discouraging times do hit, paradoxically, helps in overcoming them.

Just because I'm down doesn't mean I'll stay down. Everyone falls; the secret to staying power is comeback — getting up again. Abraham Lincoln once said to his Union Army following a defeat, "I am not so much concerned that you have fallen. I am concerned that you arise."

Lyle Schaller provides an example for pastors: "So your people are resisting relocation? Every church that relocates has resisted it at least once; maybe it will have to wait ten to twenty years. People usually say no the first time around, so leadership is all about dealing with defeat. All of us normal paranoid people will take it personally at first! So be patient and persistent."[2]

At times, I may have to do pastoral work strictly out of duty. Steve Harris remembers that one professor told him in seminary, "One of the most important lessons you can learn is that at times you'll have to minister when you don't feel like it." Once his son, Matthew, who suffers from apneic spells, stopped breathing five times in the hour before he had to perform a wedding. "As I dressed for the wedding in the hospital men's room, the last place I wanted to be was celebrating with a young couple anticipating the joys of married life," he admits. "But I also knew that I had made a commitment. The wedding went fine, although I'm sure I've done better. But the fact that I did it at all was a positive accomplishment for me. The decision to 'hang in there' is an important step for any hurting pastor."

One pastor I interviewed said to me, "I told my wife I was going to be talking to you about staying power, and she said, 'Oh, staying power is just another word for stubbornness.' "

It's both possible and rewarding to hang on in ministry. Wrote one pastor on the LEADERSHIP survey, "One resource a pastor has for staying power is the example of those who have stayed." It's helpful to hear from people who can say, as one did on the survey, "Now in retirement, the more I consider it all, the more amazed I am at the goodness of God and the loving people who have made up the membership of the churches I have served."

Knowing the potential power and sweetness of a long tenure has kept ministers going. You catch the flavor in the words of Jacob Eppinga, who came to LaGrave Avenue Christian Reformed Church in Grand Rapids, Michigan, in 1954. "The longer I stay, the better I understand the people," he says. "I'm now baptizing children whose grandparents I married. I understand the students in my catechism classes better as I see their family roots showing through. Somewhere along the line I've acquired a greater freedom just to be myself. New pastors are on their best behavior for a while, but as the years go by, you let down the façade, and people become your family. It's getting harder and harder to bury people now; they're my brothers, my sisters."

A final truth may be the hardest to keep sight of when you're discouraged: *God has used, does use, and will use my ministry.* Oswald Chambers recalls that Martin Luther cried out near the end of his life, "I am utterly weary of life. I pray the Lord will come forthwith and carry me hence." Another time Luther was dining with the Electress Dowager, and she said to him, "Doctor, I wish you may live forty years to come."

"Rather than live forty years more, I would give up my chance of Paradise," Luther replied.

"What produced the misery?" asks Chambers. "He saw the havoc the Reformation had wrought; he did not see the good; he was too near it."[3]

Pastors who have weathered discouragement have somehow been able to remind themselves of the good they have accomplished, the times when their ministry has helped people. "The time I was most discouraged in ministry, one thing that kept me going was finding indications that God had been able to use my ministry," says Ed Bratcher. "I realized there were people who felt that God had been able to use me as a pastor."

I was buoyed by answers to the question, "At what point did you experience the greatest sense of encouragement about your ministry?" on the LEADERSHIP survey. A sampling:

● "I had been working with a young person and his family. He was using drugs and was very rebellious. After a variety of incidents, late-night phone calls from him or his family, and lots of discussions, he entered treatment. Seeing him graduate with honors from that treatment center made me feel as proud as if I were his father. It gave me a sense of being in the right occupation."

● "We built a new church in a small town when it seemed an impossible though much needed undertaking. The hard work and good spirit of the building committee, the beautiful and functional finished product, and the sense of accomplishment and well-being of the congregation were encouraging."

● "The church accepted new programs in prayer ministry, family care, and outreach. Follow-through was significant, and all three programs ran with lay leadership in charge. I was encouraged because I felt like a real equipper and not the professional hired to do it all."

● "Several young people have come to Christ under my ministry and then gone into full-time Christian service. That makes it worth it all."

Events like these become life preservers, something solid to hold on to. Since God has used our ministry in the past, he will surely do so again.

God's Love

Pastor Chip Anderson of Shanesville Alliance Church in Boyertown, Pennsylvania, tells this story: "I learned a little about God's love from a phone conversation I had with my mother during a difficult and painful time in my life. I was hurting all over, and as I told my mom about my struggles, I heard some sniffling. 'Mom, are you crying?' I asked. 'A little,' she said. At that moment, no one had to tell me my mom loved me."

A balm for the discouraged pastor is realizing that God feels that hurt as well. In the words of one poet, "There is no place where earth's sorrows are felt more than up in heaven."

It's what the prophet Nahum meant when he said, "The Lord is good, a stronghold to those who are in trouble. He *knows* those who take refuge in him" (1:7). God knows what hurts us. He knows what discourages us, what brings us down. He cares, and that, countless Christians have testified, is enough.

When we're in the slough of despond, though, we often feel guilty for being there, for having fallen or waded into it. We feel dirty, unworthy of God's love. "I tend to forget that God's love isn't based on my performance, that it really is based on who I am in Christ," says Chuck Smalley of Wayzata (Minnesota) Evangelical Free Church. "I preached a sermon on grace a while back because I needed to remind myself that grace is what maintains us. It encouraged me to have to rethink that."

Says Ed Bratcher: "What helped me stay in ministry at one point was an experience I remember clearly in which Paul Tillich's phrase 'You are accepted' became real to me. I felt a release: I don't have to prove myself to God to receive his love and his mercy and his presence!"

That fragrant remembrance of God's love can sustain through the most difficult periods, as Presbyterian pastor Ben Weir found during his eighteen-month captivity in Beirut. His friend Bruce Thielemann, pastor of First Presbyterian Church in Pittsburgh, describes how Weir endured the fifteen months he was in solitary confinement:

"They took Ben into a room, a small room, and in the room there was a mattress on the floor and a radiator beside it. That was the mattress on which he slept and on which he sat, because one arm was always handcuffed to the radiator. The window had Venetian blinds. There was no other furniture. Interestingly enough there was an old stuffed bird sitting over in one corner, a poor example of the taxidermy art. There were some cracks in the walls, and where there had been a chandelier in the ceiling, it had been taken away and there were three loose wires sticking down. This was all there was in the room.

"Ben said, 'I began to use what was there to remind myself of the love of God. Those three wires coming down — well, they reminded me of the way God's hand comes down and touches the hand of Adam in Michelangelo's Sistine Chapel ceiling. You remember how the gift of life is given in such a way? This meant God's gift of life.' He counted the various slats in the Venetian blinds, and he used the Venetian blinds to remind himself that he was surrounded by a cloud of witnesses. The bird, though it was very old and dirty, he used to represent the Holy Spirit, sometimes symbolized in Scripture, as you know, by the dove.

"The cracks in the walls, the places in the plaster that were marred — each and every one of them he identified with some promise in Scripture. He would repeat to himself each day passages which he had long ago hidden in his heart: 'May the peace of God which transcends all understanding guide your heart and your mind into Christ Jesus'; 'Call upon me and I will do great and wondrous things that you know not of.'

"He remembered all of these things, and out of this he kept hold of himself for fifteen months alone — a long look, a remembering, a focusing upon the love of God."[4]

God's Call

We turn now to the third hidden resource, God's call. A "call" to ministry is not easily defined, but nothing could be more solid to most pastors. The call of God is what drew them to their work in the first place.

"Just months before I was ordained in my first charge, I was seriously contemplating becoming an academic rather than a preacher," remembers Robert Norris, pastor of Fourth Presbyterian Church in Bethesda, Maryland. "I didn't see myself as a minister; I loved the life of study. One day I was walking across the beach, deliberating the choice, when I ran across an old roommate of mine whom I hadn't seen in eleven years. He now lived in Hong Kong and was at that beach simply for the day. We began talking, I spoke with him about Christian things, and he became a believer that morning. He went back to Hong Kong knowing Christ, and I knew that I couldn't do anything else except preach the gospel for the rest of my life."

That kind of assurance has kept people in the ministry when all the circumstances pushed them to leave. One of the LEADERSHIP surveys that most struck me was from a pastor who wrote about his first pastorate. "In my gross inexperience, I just didn't know what I should do or how to deal with people," he writes. "And there was a lack of compassion and patience among the church board. They finally threatened to call for a church vote if I didn't resign, and they said they had the numbers on their side. I saw no need to try to split loyalties in our small church, so I resigned.

"I had such a strong feeling of failure — I'd failed in my job, and I'd failed God. I mean, I had just been ordained one year earlier. I began to send out resumes, thirty of them over the next ninety days, and I didn't get one response.

"I was strongly tempted to leave the ministry altogether. One of the elders in the church, who was supportive, offered me a partnership in a business of his. My salary would have doubled.

"But I finally had to tell him, 'I could do the work well, I think, but I could never be happy working any other job than the one God has called me to.' "

Because of God's call, that pastor hung on. He finally got an invitation to another church, and today both he and his church are doing well.

What happens, though, when a pastor reaches the end, when he or she cannot endure another day in ministry? What does the call of God mean for the pastor who feels, genuinely, "If I don't get out, I'm going to lose my sanity"?

Ed Bratcher wrestled with the dilemma in a previous church when he was considering leaving the ministry altogether. He'd always had a clear sense of God's call. Where was it now? What did it mean in these circumstances?

"I was forced to examine my understanding of God's call," he remembers. "I had been brought up thinking God's call was a one-time call for all time. Once you were called into a particular field or area, this was where you had to remain. To get out of the pastorate and go into any other vocation would have meant denying God's leadership.

"But gradually I began to understand that God's vocational call was not so much once-for-all-time as it was ongoing. I needed to be following his leadership not just once but always, and since he was sovereign, he might lead in different ways at different times in my life.

"That freed me a good bit. I saw that if, at that particular time, I should feel it was God's leadership to leave the pastorate, then I could do so without tremendous burden and guilt."

As it turned out, Ed sensed God's leadership was to go to another church, and he is still in the pastorate today.

For both the person who stays in pastoral ministry and the person who leaves, God's call means he is leading them and wants to use them to extend his kingdom. To sense God's leadership and to see that he is using us — that is what gives staying power.

The Once-Hidden Mystery

The apostle Paul talks frequently in Colossians of a mystery that has been hidden for ages and generations. That mystery, he explains, is the Christian's hope of glory.

What is the mysterious, long-hidden secret?

Christ in you, he says.

Christ actually dwelling within, bringing his truth, love, and call. That's what will sustain us until glory.

Pastors who've persevered have found that after all the various resources for staying power are laid out, there's still only one. Christ within.

In his second letter to the church in Corinth, Paul explains how that has kept his colleagues and him going in their ministry. "Since through God's mercy we have this ministry, we do not lose heart," he writes. "But we have this treasure in jars of clay to show that this all-surpassing power is from God and not from us. We are hard pressed on every side, but not crushed; perplexed, but not in despair; persecuted, but not abandoned; struck down, but not destroyed" (2 Cor. 4:1, 7–9).

With Christ within, Paul was able to withstand these trials and at the end of his life shout, "I have fought the good fight, I have finished the race, I have kept the faith!"

Paul's secret, our secret — the one secret — of staying power is Christ.

---

1. M. Scott Peck, *The Road Less Traveled* (New York: Simon & Schuster, 1978), 15.
2. Cited by Rowland C. Croucher, "Lyle Schaller on the Small Church," *Grid* (Autumn 1987).
3. Oswald Chambers, *Workmen of God* (Fort Washington, Penn.: Christian Literature Crusade, 1975), 65.
4. Bruce Thielemann, "Dealing with Discouragement," *Preaching Today* (48, August 1987), audiotape.